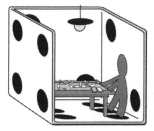

The Kobold Guide to
BOARD GAME DESIGN

By Mike Selinker

with James Ernest, Richard Garfield,
Steve Jackson, and a dozen more of the
world's best designers

OPEN DESIGN™

Credits

Lead Author and Editor: Mike Selinker

Essay Authors: Rob Daviau, James Ernest, Matt Forbeck,
Richard Garfield, Dave Howell, Steve Jackson, Richard C. Levy,
Andrew Looney, Michelle Nephew, Paul Peterson, Lisa Steenson,
Jeff Tidball, Teeuwynn Woodruff, Dale Yu

Cover Artist: John Kovalic

Proofreader: Miranda Horner

Layout: Anne Trent

Publisher: Wolfgang Baur

OPEN DESIGN LLC
P.O. Box 2811
Kirkland, WA 98083

WWW.KOBOLDQUARTERLY.COM

Foreword

We settled into Noodle Boat for a nice Thai meal. Around the table, everyone placed their orders. Asked what level of spice they wanted, the other five people each said some number of stars between one and three. The waitress then asked me.

"How many stars do you have?" I asked.

"Twenty-five," she said, earning the gasps of all present.

"Okay, I'll go with eight."

Immediately I was besieged. "Eight?!" my teammates demanded. "Why, you need to have a minimum of twelve or thirteen. Be at least half a man!"

"I don't see any of you changing your orders," I said.

"But how," the cacophony continued, "could you pick eight?"

Because I'm a *game designer*, I thought to myself. The scale that my colleagues had chosen from was, at least for pasty-faced Pacific Northwesterners, built on a scale from one to four. Everyone who walked in that door knew that scale: one was mild, four was hot. The restaurant knew that if one and four were both varieties of mild, half their customers would never return. In that game of "guess how much spice is in your food"—because, really, that's the game you play when you try a new Thai restaurant—one was low and four was high. My strategy is always the same in that game: go for high.

What I had done was expose the existence of a different game, in which four was still high but twenty-five was unimaginably high. The existence of that game did not invalidate the first game. In this new game, I played conservatively. And let me tell you, eight was *hot*. Many Scovilles died to make that meal. Because I had a very spicy dinner that still had flavor and nuance, I won that game.

The people who you'll find in the pages of this book know how to play and win games such as this. That's because they design them. In here you'll find the designers of many of your favorite games, and a few whose games you might not have heard of, but should, because they're awesome. They also can write, which is not a given with game designers. They know whereof they speak.

By the end of this book, you will also know whereof they speak. That's because they're all willing to tell you how they work. If you want a career like theirs, you could do a lot worse than following their leads. I've collaborated with all of them in one capacity or another. If you're lucky, you will too.

In the course of these essays, we'll cover many subjects. Some are more philosophical—how to think, how to prepare, how to evaluate. Some are more practical—how to playtest, how to balance, how to prototype. But wherever they fall on that axis, all matter. If you take the time at each step of your design process to consider each writer's words, by your last step you will have done everything better.

The Kobold-in-Chief, Wolfgang Baur, wanted a selection of designers with wildly differing experiences and voices. Some are mass market and some are hobby. Some have stayed within one field and others have done a little bit of everything. They often disagree with each other. You might wonder how you will choose between the advice of one and the advice of another. You're smart. You'll figure it out.

But enough promises. Let's get to work.

Mike Selinker

Seattle, Washington

Contents

Part 3: Development 73

Part 4: Presentation 107

Part 1
Concepting

In which we figure out what games to make, who will play those games, and what impressions we will leave them with.

The Game Is Not the Rules

by James Ernest

Mike here. It's my job, as compiler and editor of this book, to give you an understanding of what will be in the book, whose job is to give you an understanding of what the game design process is like. So I'm doing that by getting out of the way. I'm going to introduce you to some of the finest minds in the business, with a little paragraph like this one in front of each essay. We'll start with a topic-setting essay by James Ernest, my primary board and card game design partner. He said what follows way better than I could. Listen up.

A game is a way to play by a set of rules. Good rules help you find the fun. Bad rules obscure it. But the rules are not, themselves, the fun. It sounds obvious when you say it like that. But game designers of all skill levels fall into the trap of believing that the mechanics and the game are the same thing.

A game is a whole package. It is not a collection of parts. A game can have a theme, a mechanic, a brand, a hook, a lifestyle. But these parts are not interchangeable with other games. It's only as a complete unit that the game resonates, draws attention, engages players, and becomes a part of their lives.

If you want to invent a new game, you have to do better than just improving on existing rules. You need to consider why the game, as a whole, will get into players' heads.

"COMPELLING GAME MECHANICS"

Recently I was on a panel of game experts at a local gaming convention. Someone in the audience asked, "What would you consider to be compelling game mechanics?" I had to answer, "There is something wrong with your question."

Game mechanics are like the parts of a watch. What would you consider to be compelling watch parts? I could tell you about bridges, wheels, and springs all day. But you'd be no closer to understanding what makes a "good watch." Nobody buys a watch because of its gears. Even the people who say they do.

Game mechanics are like watch gears. A "compelling" game mechanic only makes sense in context. Transplant that mechanic into another game, and there is no guarantee that it will work.

This is not to say that games can't borrow mechanics from each other. They certainly do. But blindly transplanting pieces from one mechanism to another is a terrible way to design. You can't just throw a bunch of random watch pieces together and expect them to tell time. You must have a plan.

When you break a game down into its component parts, you can certainly learn about that game. But you can't apply very much of what you've learned toward creating a new one. Breaking something down into components really only teaches you about the components; it obscures your perception of the whole. A map of Spain tells you very little about the New World.

THE CRITICAL APPROACH

It's hard to be a creator when all you have is critical skill. That's why the jobs of critic and creator rarely overlap.

If I ask the question "all good watches are (blank)," what do you say? The whiteboard is empty. Begin.

They have hands. They have a face. They have numbers. They are precise. Accurate. Fashionable. Affordable. They tell time. Uh, they have gears. They use electricity. They have an alarm. And so on.

Keep throwing things out there, and I'm sure I can think of a counterexample for each one. A watch without hands, for example. And I can also think of something that is not a watch that has most of these things. In fact, a varsity football player makes it most of the way through the list.

Did that get us anywhere? It depends. We've thoroughly defined "watch," but we aren't much closer to making a new one. Hitting everything on the checklist is no guarantee of being good. And plenty of watches have little in common with the list.

The player is the consumer of the game. It's his opinion you should really be courting. What makes someone buy a new watch? Functionality. Practicality. Fashion. People buy watches to express who they are. Even if "who they are" is summed up as "I bought a cheap watch because I don't care to express who I am through my choice of watch."

So to make a new watch, you have to consider aspects of the marketplace and the mind of the consumer. The mechanics of the watch are basically a given. Getting a customer to notice you has almost nothing to do with that.

Games are the same, only (I think) more complicated. In part, the job of analyzing and defining game is harder because it's not as easy to see the moving parts. When a game-maker does his job correctly, most of the moving parts are invisible, even when you break open the case.

And games have this weird albatross word that, I would guess, watches don't have. That word is "fun." I don't think a watchmaker feels like he has to make his watch "fun," though some clearly do. When we try to define "fun" we usually spin our wheels for a while, and then we realize that we are just recapitulating the process of defining "game," and we're back where we started.

Okay, kids. "All games are (blank)." Begin.

They are fun. They have players. They have rules. They have a board. Or cards. Or dice. Or some kind of pieces. Or not, I guess. They have a finite play time. They have a winner and a loser. They have turns. Or phases. Yeah, the good games have phases. They have luck. Sometimes. They have strategy. Sometimes. They are replayable. Or at least, they should be….

And yes, the same thing I said about the watch list applies here too: I can think of a counterexample for every one of these, and I can also think of things that aren't "games" that hit most of these marks. Like maybe a disco.

What does all this mean? Let me restate my premise: I don't think you can learn how to invent a new game by smashing an old game and measuring the pieces. All that tells you is how to make a copy of it. Maybe your version will be an incremental improvement, and maybe not. But it won't be new.

Fine. So, analysis won't lead to ingenuity. In that case, what will?

YOUR TWO BRAINS

You have two brains. They are the child brain and the adult brain. They represent the creative and the critical sides of your personality.

The child brain is the fun brain. He's eager. Trusting. Everything is magical and new. The child brain likes robots and zombies and pirates. He knows when an idea is good. You should trust him on that. But he lacks discipline. He's not very good at finishing things.

The adult brain is the boring one. She's the critic. Everything you can think of has been done before, and she's first in line to tell you. The adult brain constantly steps in and reminds the child brain that there have already been plenty of games about zombies, and the world doesn't need another one, no matter how cool they are.

When you're coming up with an idea for a new game, you need to tell your adult brain to shut up. It's hard. The adult sounds like the smart one. But she doesn't have a clue whether an idea is really good, or just a version of something she's seen before.

Imagine yourself in a pitch meeting. Each time you throw out a new idea, it gets shot down. If someone in the room has heard of something like it, they say, "We can't use that; it's already been done." If no one has heard of anything like it, they say, "I just can't see how that will work." Not one idea is given the chance to develop into something new. I have the luxury of not having to imagine this meeting, because I can remember it.

Gamers are, unfortunately, dominated by their adult brains. They can talk themselves into anything. So if you're a gamer who wants to be a game designer, you have to re-learn how to think. Let yourself be passionate. Don't second-guess every idea. Be a child.

Children are enthusiastic. They are naïve. They can take an idea and run with it. And they have zero baggage. They are genuinely unaware that what they are thinking of has been done before, and this is the kind of mindset that allows them to start from somewhere familiar and get somewhere new.

My daughter came up to me this morning and told me that she had a dream about an adventure in the Amazon. Her team got in a bloody fight with lions. And then they became the cast of *Scooby-Doo* and solved a mystery. I had the same thought you did: "There are no lions in the Amazon." But I didn't say it, because I wanted to hear the rest of the dream.

In the brainstorming phase of your game, the adult needs to shut up. Otherwise, you will never hear the rest of the dream.

Once the child has made something he can really fall in love with, the adult can come back to the table. Her job is to look at the project and figure out whether it's delivering on the basic definition of the project. The scope, the audience, the marketplace. Things the child doesn't care about.

Critical thinking enters the game design process once the creative mind has already settled on what it wants. Write those goals down. Be clear. Stick to them. If your game isn't working, this is the time to measure it against what you know: other games, game theory, math, science, reason. But you can steer this thing correctly only if the goals, the child's ideas, are clearly established.

ENGAGEMENT

If I had to pick one thing that games should have, I'd call it "engagement." That's a tough term. I basically mean "a reason to play." I don't like to say "a hook" because that implies superficiality. It's not just a foot in the door; it's the reason you keep coming back. It's what distinguishes a hit from a flop, between two games that are empirically identical.

Engagement can happen for a lot of reasons, and (this is the hardest part) players can't always explain why. If you ask a *Magic* player why he likes the game, he will tell you about the game mechanics, and list his favorite cards, and bore you with tournament anecdotes. But what he probably won't tell you is "*Magic* makes me feel smart."

Everything in that game, including the play of hands, the construction of decks, and the buying and reselling of cards, makes players feel smart. It feeds their need to be intellectually superior to each other, to the game designers, and to the marketplace. This isn't bad. It's great. It's fun to feel smart. But there are very similar games out there in terms of mechanics, card abilities, and tournament anecdotes. The reasons he is giving you are not exactly right.

Popular games are like this. Complain all you want about the mechanics of *Monopoly*. That game works. People don't play it for its mechanics. They play it because it's familiar, easy, and because they want to pretend to be rich. People don't play charades to show off their knowledge of movies, books, and celebrities. They do it because they like watching their friends embarrass themselves. People don't play *Dungeons & Dragons* because they love adventure. They do it because they believe their social group will fall apart without some kind of structure.

Now ask yourself, why do I like the games I like? And what kind of emotions do I want to create in my players? Forget about starting with your favorite game mechanic, or your favorite theme. Start with a concise expression of how you want your players to feel. And "I want them to have fun" doesn't cut it. There are different kinds of fun.

There is nothing compelling about game mechanics. There is something compelling about games. Games engage players on a gut level that they are barely aware of. As a designer, you must be aware of the real reasons that people will want to play your games, even if they will never notice it themselves.

And when they compliment you on your excellent rules, just smile and say "thank you."

James Ernest is best known as the force behind Seattle's Cheapass Games, publishers of dozens of games like Kill Doctor Lucky, Button Men, Brawl, and Give Me the Brain. His non-Cheapass games include Pirates of the Spanish Main, Gloria Mundi, and Lords of Vegas. He has also designed casual computer games for Microsoft and Gazillion. He is the author of the book Contact Juggling and the co-author of Dealer's Choice: The Complete Handbook of Saturday Night Poker, and is a frequent guest lecturer at game conventions and design schools.

Play More Games

by Richard Garfield

In some parallel universe, there's a Richard Garfield who invented the game Magic: The Gathering, *and then rested on his laurels. That's a pretty strange universe, because the Richard Garfield I've known for the last couple decades doesn't know how to do that. Richard is constantly and professorially poking at the beast that is game design, seeing what makes it purr and what makes it roar. A key element of that inquiry is a willingness to play anything that moves. Here's Richard on the subject of game research.*

People who wish to design games should play games. Lots of them.

There are designers who say they don't play other people's games because they are afraid the concepts therein will infiltrate their design. They believe in design in a vacuum. Imagine a world where Steven Spielberg didn't watch films, Stephen King didn't read anything, and Stephen Hawking didn't consider anyone's science but his own. Do you think their craft would be better? In that world I don't believe we would even know their names.

Isaac Newton famously claimed he could see further because he was standing on the shoulder of giants, and in fact, there are no cultural advances in a vacuum—whether art or science. Why should games be any different? While there are some successful designers that maintain an attitude of minimizing outside influence for fear of being "contaminated," I can only believe that their games would be better if they embraced and built upon the wonderful tradition of games and the work of their contemporaries. Their decision is made to showcase their personal design talent at the cost of the game's quality.

"Fine," you say. "I am designing board games, so I will play board games." To this I say, "Not enough!" You should play board games, card games, electronic games, sports, arcade games, roleplaying games, miniature games, wargames, mathematical games, party games, puzzle hunts, and casino games. You should watch game shows, sporting events, and game championships. Great design may incorporate ideas from all games.

To see how important playing very different games can be, one has to look no farther than roleplaying games. The granddaddy of roleplaying games is *Dungeons & Dragons*. Its designers, Gary Gygax and Dave Arneson, couldn't play roleplaying games—they didn't exist. They were military wargame and miniatures enthusiasts, and those roots strongly influence many roleplaying games. It is quite likely that most roleplayers today have never even played a wargame, let alone made a hobby of it. The roots of great games often lie in surprising places, and sometimes so far afield that the players won't ever run into them casually. Your games will be improved if you have the capability of sowing your design seeds far and wide.

If you don't like a game that is popular, you should take responsibility for figuring out why people like it. Play with those people—watch them and understand that they are not wrong to like the game. A pleasant side effect of understanding why people like a particular game is that you will appreciate it, and maybe even end up liking it—something that will make your life richer.

Take for example *Monopoly*, a game which modern designers love to hate. There is so much wrong with *Monopoly* according to modern sensibility that designers tend to credit its ongoing success entirely to quirks of history. A few of the observations you may make if you play the game with fans and an open mind:

- Players really like the building aspect of the game. Monopoly was one of the first games that allowed players to accumulate and nurture resources, making it appeal to the "builder" player.
- Players are invested in a game that they can be eliminated from. If you aren't playing for money, what are your stakes? Just as money adds spice to the game, elimination does as well. Modern game design weighs elimination so negatively that it loses track of what it does for a game.
- Players are invested in other player's turns. In many roll-and-move games, a player's turn is the only interesting thing to the player. So playing a game with three other players means only 25% of the game is interesting. In *Monopoly*, the best things happen on other player's turns.

There are lessons like these in any popular game, even the ones that we don't immediately like or think are "bad." Use the explanation "the players don't know any better" as sparingly as possible.

Games that aren't popular can be learned from as well—why do the fans like the game despite the characteristics that keep it from being more broadly popular? In your design, could you incorporate features that those fans like so much without the characteristics that drive other players away?

One of my favorite games, *Titan*, might fall into this category. Why do fans like it despite the fact that the game lasts an unpredictable but often very long time, players can be eliminated, and players can often be doing nothing for half an hour or more? The feeling that you are building something distinctive is quite strong in *Titan*—perhaps that is part of it. But my favorite characteristic is the way there is strong interaction in the game without it devolving into "picking on the winner." Most modern design either has much less interaction or are much more political in the way players decide who to conflict with. Also, perhaps some of the negative characteristics, like the elimination, are not as bad as we think.

At what point should you worry that your design may be leaning too heavily on another design? This is often a tough question, but if the players are genuinely getting something out of your game that isn't in the other, you are probably on safe ground. If you look closely at any design, it looks like nothing is original, but that doesn't validate the conclusion that all designs are unoriginal. A meal is more than its ingredients. A piece of music is more than a list of notes. It is the way the designer holistically combines design elements that matters.

In fact, beginning designers often *over*-innovate. One of the wonderful things about games is how much they can give a player—a good game can give pleasure for a lifetime. But that combined with the fact that learning new games is difficult makes it so we really have to work hard to get people to try new games. Some innovation is certainly called for—that will entice the players—but too much makes the games hard to learn. Every unusual building block, every break in what the players regard as a standard is not only an opportunity to entice, it is also an opportunity to confuse, and hence raise the bar to enter. A designer should take responsibility for making sure that every significant departure from the norm is worth the player's time to learn. If a designer doesn't know the standard, the designer cannot determine if it is worth the cost to the player.

Excellent games are often thought to be much more innovative than they actually are. Consider the reputation of a company like Blizzard. They make excellent games, but they do far more perfection of existing game forms than they do innovation within those forms. *Starcraft* and *World of Warcraft* are perfect games for a large audience, but hardly as innovative as the first RTS, which might be *Dune 2*, or as earlier graphical MMORPGs, like *Ultima Online* or *Everquest*.

As a designer you should understand your influences and, I believe, credit them. Understanding them will make you a better designer, and crediting them will nurture the design community in a number of ways. Designers trying to improve their craft will understand more, and look for their own inspirations. Designers who may not even have had success with their design at least get peer recognition for some of their ideas. Also, these design ties make the building blocks with which we can build a historical understanding of games. Games prior to the 1900s were notoriously poorly documented—and even today we come nowhere close to the documentation and critique that, say, literature or music has. Understanding and sharing your influences is probably the best you can do to help that if you don't actually want to become a game historian for us.

An example of how this influence might play out can be seen in my game *King of Tokyo*. The game is built on the mechanics of *Yahtzee*. I was thinking about *Yahtzee* because I played the *Catan Dice Game*, and was impressed by the play space that Klaus Teuber was exploring. I don't think I was directly influenced by *Catan Dice*, but without playing it I may never have returned to *Yahtzee* and asked myself how to make that game more interactive. The flavor of the game is influenced by the board game *The Creature That Ate Sheboygan* and the electronic game *Crush, Crumble, and Chomp!* There are sure to be many influences that have been so assimilated into my design I no longer recognize them. *King of Tokyo* wouldn't exist if I didn't play a wide variety of games, old and new, and think critically about them. And yet I am confident no one who plays it will consider it derivative. And if they do, I will blow them up with my Nova Breath.

One should play games for more than just research, one should play because it is fun. And if it isn't fun you should question your desire to make them. During the times in my life that I haven't had time to play, my design has suffered; it felt drier and more rote. I am sure there are ways to discipline your way through these times, but for me it has worked better to find the time to play—I immediately get back in touch with the joy of games and that is reflected in my design.

Join me on the shoulder of giants, the view is great—play games, learn from them, enjoy them, and one day designers will stand on our shoulders.

Richard Garfield designed the first trading card game, Magic: The Gathering, in 1993. This former math professor has published half a dozen other TCG designs, as well board and card games such as Filthy Rich, What Were You Thinking?, King of Tokyo, and Let's Jet. He consults on game design with companies such as Microsoft, Electronic Arts, and The Pokémon Company. He teaches a "Characteristics of Games" class, the material for which has been made into a textbook published by MIT Press.

Pacing Gameplay

Three-Act Structure Just Like God and Aristotle Intended

by Jeff Tidball

Everybody in this book knows how to write, but only one of us was trained to do so at USC's School of Cinematic Arts. Jeff was, and that might be why his games seem like fully developed stories. When I first held his Pieces of Eight *in my hand—see, it's just a set of coins, so it all fits in your hand—I could feel the solid weight of a complete story clanking between my fingers. A pirate captain masters a ship, he sails it amid danger-filled waters, he rallies his scalawags, and sends his foes to Davy Jones's Locker. Jeff did that with coins. I asked Jeff to tell us about how a game builds like a story.*

YOU MAY HAVE HEARD OF ARISTOTLE.

A while ago, Aristotle wrote a treatise called *Poetics* about how drama works. One of the most important things he wrote in it is how a decent plot for anything dramatic has a beginning, a middle, and an end.

Aristotle was on to something. Thinking about stories in terms of their beginnings, middles, and ends helps shine a light on how stories function, especially in terms of their pacing. It helps explain why some stories are compelling and other stories are more like *X-Men 3*.

As a separate matter, our minds store, recall, and understand the happenings of life as stories whether they're events of total inconsequence or critical importance. A phone call distracted me and my toast burned. Rome expanded to encompass too diverse a territory and so it declined and fell. We remember things about the world in the form of dramas writ small, writ large, or writ in-between. That's part of the reason we find anecdotal evidence so compelling even though it's the worst kind of data there is. An anecdote is a story, and our brains love stories.

The playing of a game—like the making of toast or the collapsing of the Roman Empire—is also experienced by players as a story about what happened. You cornered the market on sheep, you built a sheep port, you connected all that with the longest road, and you proceeded to steamroll all who opposed you.

The point is this: It's fruitful to consider the experience of playing games in terms of the story of the player's gameplay. To come at it from a slightly different angle, the best way to understand a game's pacing is to think about how the player experiences gameplay as the story of what he did.

What's more, it's extremely fruitful to examine players' stories of gameplay in terms of those stories' beginnings, middles, and ends—which is to say, their three-act structure. If you use those insights to build and fine-tune gameplay that exploits folks' hardwired expectations about what's in a good story's beginning, its middle, and its end, your game will be made of win.

DIVIDING STORIES INTO ACTS IS PRIMARILY AN ANALYTICAL EXERCISE.

This is theory we're talking about here. As such, it is useful to creators to the extent that it helps them analyze their works-in-progress and improve them. An analytic, theoretical framework helps us talk about what is common, what is unusual, what is successful, and what is a godforsaken disaster.

A theory does not, however, help creators do the raw act of creation. A theory about hammers is different from hammering. If that doesn't make sense to you, go build a house real quick using nothing but your theory about hammers. I'll be here when you get—

—oh, back already? Very good. Moving on....

EVERYONE HAS A DIFFERENT IDEA ABOUT WHAT EACH ACT IS FOR.

The realm of Platonic ideals does not contain examples of the consummate first act, the flawless second act, and the ideal third act. Aristotle defined them in a way that made sense for Greek tragedies because he thought *Oedipus Rex* was a pretty swell play. Syd Field took a different approach and made a lot of money selling his book to would-be moviemakers.

Playwrights, novelists, and screenwriters; their critics; and countless academics have proposed myriad variations on what makes a good first act, what belongs in a second act, and what constitutes a third act. Others don't even agree that there are three acts. Some propose five, or six. Teleplays have functional act breaks for commercials as well as dramatic act breaks. (Sometimes they even fall in the same place.)

Aristotle. Syd Field. *Pfft.* Let me tell you what I think:

A story's first act sets the stage.

It introduces the characters. It brings their situation to the point where a dramatic question is posed that the audience cares about enough to endure the rest of the story.

A story's second act answers the dramatic question.

Through twists and turns, the audience is made to wonder what the dramatic question's answer will be. Ultimately, the second act of a well-formed story answers the dramatic question once and for all, for happy or sad.

A story's third act tells the audience what happens as a result.
Maybe it's about what happens in the world, maybe it's about what happens to the hero, or maybe it's about what happens to some framing narrator who didn't have a personal stake in the dramatic question at all. The story's third act's real point is to put what the audience just experienced in a context that gives it meaning for them in the real world.

Put your hand down in the back row.

It doesn't matter whether my pet idea of how a story's beginning, middle, and end function is Good, Right, and True because we're going to talk about gameplay now.[1] The important thing to understand before we move on is that a story has a beginning, a middle, and an end, and that each part serves a different function, and that the transitions between them are Important because they establish the story's pacing, whether the viewer or reader is consciously aware of it or not. We're constantly and instinctively on the lookout for these transitions. We anticipate them. We look forward to them. We get kinda pissed off when they're missing.

The changes in a story's tone and tenor as its acts unfold clue us in to when we're supposed to put our popcorn down and pay attention, whether we can hold off going to the bathroom until the thing's over, if we'd better call the babysitter because we're going to be here a while. There's little that makes an audience crankier than when their expectations about the kinds of things that are supposed to be happening at this point in the story aren't being met.

The "story" of gameplay can be thought of in an act-based way.

Gameplay's first act—its beginning—is when the stage is set for conflict among the players. Battle lines are drawn and the players understand the dimensions of the conflict.

Gameplay's second act—its middle—is the meat of the struggle for victory. Each player constantly strives to establish a compelling and enduring edge over the others, so he can make a final push for victory.

Gameplay's third act—its end—is the push for victory. One player, or several players in succession, either try and fail or try and ultimately succeed in sealing the deal and ending the game with their own victory.

Hopefully these different descriptions of gameplay states resonate naturally with your experience of playing games. If this mode of analysis has any merit for you, you're already nodding your head, recognizing these as ways you've felt at various points in many games you've played in your life.

---

[1] If the way acts are defined for dramatic stories interests you, I suggest *The Tools of Screenwriting*, by David Howard and Edward Mabley. Lots of people like Robert McKee's *Story* instead; that dude is loaded. And *Poetics* is, of course, still in print, and available for free all around the web.

Hopefully, also, you see almost immediately how this approach to gameplay pacing can explain why some games are no damn fun. In some games, no stage is set. In others, the game ends before anyone realizes they should be pushing for victory. At times, the endgame drags on interminably because no one can win.

Let's talk more about each of those acts.

The first act draws battle lines.

Many games have a game-space that's larger—sometimes much larger—than the scope of the real meat of the struggle. This can be literal, as in a wargame where victory in World War II will be decided in Poland, never mind that the map covers the extent of Europe. Or, it can be conceptual, or mechanical. In a given play or a particular game, the real meat of the conflict might be bounded by an initiative mechanic that establishes which player will have a critical advantage of timing (never mind that the game has many other mechanics), or defined by resource acquisition (never mind that the victory condition involves winning battles).

The first act ends when it becomes clear to savvy players that the boundaries of the conflict have been pretty well established, and when they therefore get a concrete grasp on what they'll be trying to accomplish for the main portion of the game's remaining length.[2] The victory conditions have moved beyond the way the rulebook expresses them ("win by holding three capitals") to instead relate each player's specific plan for victory ("I'll probably win by taking over Foo, Bar, and the Vatican City State").

Ideally, the first act helps new players understand how the rules of the game work, so they can approach the second act with confidence that they're on an even footing with the other players, at least in their mechanical understanding of play. Games where understanding key rules takes longer are especially punishing to pick up.

No player should feel like they are—or should actually be—eliminated from consideration for victory in the game's first act. A game where something can go that drastically wrong for anyone in the first act is deeply flawed. *Dune*, for example.

Though the phrase "set up" is used ubiquitously in methods of story analysis to describe first acts in general, a game's setup—the taking from its box and assembly on the table—is not part of its gameplay's first act. Nice try, though, *Arkham Horror*.

---

[2] An interesting area of inquiry past the scope of this essay might revolve around the question of whether players can set in motion "additional" second acts by struggling to redefine the act's frame to favor their own victory. Strategically, this is probably very sensible. But most players will only have so much patience for constant redefinition of the game's core. If the chief struggle is shifting sand, the gameplay's story becomes one of frustration and groundlessness.

The second act is the meat of gameplay.

In the second act, the players struggle against one another to get to the point where they can make a credible stab at victory.

Only players who are not remotely paying attention should be confused about what they should be trying to do in the second act of gameplay. Players may be horribly, terribly *tempted* to do other things, either by devious mechanics or by the clever strategery of the other players. But the battle lines having been drawn, the players will have the most fun pressing the battle rather than meandering confusedly from game mechanic to game mechanic.

In good games, the players will directly oppose each other in their second act struggles. Cooperative games seem like an exception but aren't; they simply require the understanding that the players constitute a bloc allied together on one side of a battle line drawn against the game itself. Ditto for solitaire games.

In the very best games, there will be many opportunities for different players to trade what looks to all of them like the leading position. A game that at any point looks like a foregone conclusion isn't fun. Even the leader in a runaway game only has fun when said leader has that odious personality defect that allows someone to be entertained by mercilessly crushing opponents. Which isn't to say that you've got to give away points when you're winning or else you're an ass. It's to point out that all of the players should want an exciting game as well as want to win, and it's to point out that excitement arises primarily from not knowing whether you're going to win. You keep playing to find out.

The third act is the push for victory, the endgame.

We had a saying in my game group when I was in college: "If Joe's not stopped, he's going to win the game!" Inevitably, at some point, as we neared a given game's close, it became clear that Joe was going to win the game. Again. It was at this point that everyone else banded together to try to stop him from winning. Which usually didn't work.[3]

The second act transitions to the third act at the point where it becomes clear to the savvy player that one of the players has achieved a clear upper hand, and that barring a reversal of some kind, that player is going to win.

The accompanying emotional alarm (or euphoria, depending) is the key to the third act. All of the players know that the end is near, and that they've either got to take one last stab at unseating the leader or they've just got to hang in there for a little while longer to secure their triumph.

---

[3] I hereby enlist you—yes, you—in the sacred fraternity of those allied to prevent Joe from winning the game. But I digress.

A player's successes and failures in the second act should obviously be the massive determining factor in whether he's the third act's frontrunner for victory. If that's not the case, then the game is probably…um…what's the opposite of good, again?

A key feature of an emotionally satisfying third act, though, is that the frontrunner's victory must not be inevitable. If it's inevitable, the whole third act is an unnecessary mechanical exercise. And that's bad, because remember, we consciously or subconsciously really, really want the story to have a satisfying end. So, in the third act, it should still be possible—though perhaps very, very difficult—for other players, and ideally *any* other player, to still snatch victory from the jaws of defeat. As soon as a player realizes he can't possibly win, the game stops being fun because the emotional tension drains away. This can go truly sideways if functionally eliminated players can still exert influence on which other player does win. You know this as the kingmaker effect. It's the opposite of good.

At some point in the third act, one player must make a stab at victory *that actually results in victory.* For a designer or publisher, a seemingly endless endgame is even more terrible than it might appear, because its actual tedium is magnified in the players' minds because their experience of the game ended on that note. Ever played a game where you didn't care who won as long as the bloody thing was over? Yeah, that.

I HAVE THREE ADDITIONAL THOUGHTS ABOUT ALL OF THIS:

Thought the first:
In films, the places where acts meet each other are often quite clear. A particular event transpires and is clearly a bright line of transition. Terrorists take over at the Nakatomi Plaza, say. Analyzing gameplay is more difficult, in part because each play of the game must be separately considered. It seems likely to me that act transitions in gameplay are more gradual than they are in plays, stories, and films. That players ease more slowly from one act into another in games. When thinking about your own work, it's fruitful to consider whether gradual or sudden transitions are more fun, and tailor your design accordingly. It's also fruitful to consider whether mechanics that change over the game's unfolding acts could help, or hurt, the game's pacing as the players experience it. That is, do you want to highlight those transitions, or conceal them?

Thought the second:
An act-based framework for analyzing roleplaying games, or even board and card games that tell stories, would look different from this framework. Such analyses would have to take those games' narrative into account, as opposed to the players' experience of their gameplay. This model is entirely divorced from whatever veneer of setting that's coupled to the game mechanics. An RPG

scenario, or Ameritrash board game, might even have three acts to describe its story that are entirely divorced from the three acts that delineate its gameplay. I leave it to someone else to decide whether a correspondence between the two would be desirable, irrelevant, or something else.

Thought the third:

It seems to me that Eurogames often go wrong by only having a second act. Discuss.

I SEE THAT YOU'RE HEADED FOR YOUR COMPUTER TO RANT ON YOUR BLOG.

No, not about the Euro slam.[4] You're headed to your blog to point out that this analytical method has no merit because no designer has ever designed a game with this three-act structure in mind.

And, yes: I don't believe a structural division into acts has been proposed for gameplay before. I've never seen one, anyway. People have written about the stories in story-based games and talked about act divisions, but when they have, they've been talking about dividing the game's story up, not the game's gameplay.

So let me reiterate this crucial point: The whole question of division into acts is a theoretical and analytical tool, not a builder's tool. It is a method of evaluating a blueprint or improving a first draft, not a method of pounding nails. The theoretical blog post or forum rant rebutting the very idea of an act-based analysis of gameplay because no designer has ever designed a board or card game with act breaks in mind falls down because grown-ups are allowed to interpret creative works outside their designers' intentions. In point of fact, smart designers proactively seek such points of broader perspective on their own work because it allows them to make such intention-free interpretations, and thereby improve their material.

THE POINT IS ANALYTICAL, BUT THE POINT IS TO MAKE BETTER GAMES.

The idea behind a three-act framework for considering the pacing of gameplay is not to provide three boxes into which different mechanics should be put, or to divide a 120-minute playing time into arbitrary segments and then argue about whether we've put the signposts in the right places. Rather, I hope that understanding the pacing of gameplay in terms of a three-act structure can help designers understand players' unconscious expectations, and as a reflection of that understanding, make better games without resorting to blind, hit-or-miss guesswork.

---

[4] On that point rant away, though it's fair to warn you that I can't hear you, having, as I do, my fingers in my ears.

My guess is that this set of ideas will be especially helpful to designers and developers troubleshooting designs where playtesting has revealed that the mechanics are working as intended but no one is having fun, or enough fun. In fact, since I wrote the first outline for this essay, this approach has already improved the design for one of the games I'm working on at the moment. By that standard, the idea is successful already.

Jeff Tidball *is a freelance game designer whose credits include Pieces of Eight, Cthulhu 500, and Fantasy Flight Games' edition of Horus Heresy. He's the co-author, with Will Hindmarch, of Things We Think About Games. He has been Vice President of Product Development at Fantasy Flight Games, holds an MFA in Screenwriting from the University of Southern California, and has located his website at jefftidball.com.*

Metaphor vs. Mechanics

Don't Fight the Fusion
by Matt Forbeck

There are lots of reasons Matt Forbeck might say no to a game design project—time, money, a need to get his quadruplets to soccer practice—but a lack of familiarity with the game type will not be among them. Matt has written every kind of thing that thingmakers make. He imbues everything he touches with personality, using his unrivaled knowledge of why something should read or sound or think the way it does. When you read his work, you will hear him talking. You'll like that sound, I promise. Here, Matt tells us how he makes each of his games greater than the sum of its parts.

When many game designers sit down to tackle a new project, they aim at it from one of two angles. They either figure out the mechanics first or go straight for the metaphor instead.

For our purposes, the mechanics include the hard and fast rules that make the game tick, the stuff you work with as you play the game. The metaphor is what the game is supposedly about.

For example, the mechanics of *Monopoly* include: rolling two dice and adding the results together to determine how many squares you must move your pawn around the board; using points (in the form of fake money) to establish advantages over other players, transfer power between players, keep score, and determine the end of the game; the board itself, including the placement of various features around the track that bounds it; and the rules for trading advantages (properties).

In *Monopoly*, the metaphor is that each player is a capitalist who sets out to make himself rich at the expense of those around him. You win the game by accumulating all of the wealth in the game and bankrupting everyone else.

The mechanics are the abstract means by which the game works. The metaphor is the game's beautiful lie, the fiction that gives the game context and a broader meaning.

So, which is more important? Which should you start with to give yourself the best game?

Neither, silly.

MAKING YOUR GAME PURR

A game is a complex conglomerate of many elements, including art, rules, components, mechanics, and metaphor. Think of each of these elements as a piston in a car's engine. A game can limp along with the pistons coughing or knocking along out of sequence, but for it to really hum you need to be firing on all pistons in perfect sync with each other.

A game without mechanics isn't a game. It's a story. Or possibly a thought experiment.

A game without a metaphor isn't a game. It's a math problem. Maybe a puzzle. Or a toy.

Even the most abstract games wear at least a veneer of metaphor. That gives the players a way to wrap our minds around the various mechanics and give them meaning.

The most famous abstract game of all—by which I mean, something that concentrates on mechanics rather than story—is chess, a game in which you move stylized pieces around a grid of squares to emulate a battle between two kingdoms vying for power. You could play it without any metaphor at all, but it would lose most of its meaning. Why can the knight move the way it does? What's all this about castling? Why does a bishop move at oblique angles? How come pawns start so weak but can advance in power?

So as a game designer, where do you start? With the mechanics or the metaphor?

That's entirely up to you, and it can change from game to game, depending on the circumstances.

THE MECHANICAL METHOD

Sometimes a great mechanic or a component comes along, and you decide you just have to make a game out of it. Maybe it's the idea of a card game that's sold in packs of cards randomly selected from a much larger set, like *Magic: The Gathering*. Or maybe it's a fantastic component, like a headband you can wear to mentally control the movement of a ball, as in *Mind Flex*.

In any case, once you have that singular element, you can start to build a game around it, but don't mistake that element for the game itself. Games of even moderate complexity require a number of different mechanics working together in symphony. And if you strive for elegance in your game design— intuitive rules that hang together in a way that makes them both memorable and sensible—your mechanics should all work together seamlessly.

Once you're done with the mechanics, you have the bare bones of a game, the skeleton on which you can now throw some flesh. A good set of mechanics can be used in conjunction with all sorts of metaphors. Just look at Richard Borg's *Command and Colors* rules, which have served as the basis for *Memoir '44*, *Battle Cry*, and a number of other excellent games. Or at Steve Jackson Games's *GURPS*, literally the *Generic Universal RolePlaying System*, which has had dozens of setting (metaphor) supplements published for it over its decades in print.

The great thing about having a sturdy set of mechanics is that if a player learns them once, they know the bulk of the rules for every other game that includes those mechanics. It reduces the learning load for the players and makes it easier for them to pick up a new game. At their heart, though, most games represent an abstraction of a complex situation. That means that even generic, reusable rules eventually need to be tailored to the specific metaphor or setting to which you transplant them.

THINKING METAPHORICALLY

To nail your game's metaphor, try reducing it to its essentials. Take some time to consider what your game is about. Write it down. Keep it less than a paragraph. If you can make it a single sentence, that's ideal. Try the following format:

> [Game name] is a [category of] game in which [the players or their avatars] [do or compete for something] by [using tools the game provides them].

For example:

- *Monopoly* is a board game in which landlords strive to drive each other bankrupt by purchasing and improving properties and charging the highest rents they can.
- *Magic: The Gathering* is a collectible card game in which powerful wizards duel to the death with each other by tapping the magical power of the lands around them and using magic to do battle with their foes.
- *Trivial Pursuit* is a board game in which players compete to answer questions in six different categories before the others by testing each other with cards filled with trivia questions.

Once you've done this, you should have at least a good idea about the silhouette of your final game. From there, you just need to fill it in from the edges.

METAPHORS AND LICENSES

In many ways, it's easier to design a game based around an existing metaphor. If someone hands you a licensed property to work with, something based on a TV show, film, book, comic, song, or whatever, all the hard part's been done for you, right? The story's already there.

But even then, you have to figure out what's so incredible about the original story and then hope you can translate that into a game. Every medium is different, and things that work wonderfully in one don't always translate well to another. (Just ask anyone who's loved a book but hated the film based on it.) The interpersonal dramas of a comic book series like *X-Men*, for instance, are harder to model in a board game than a superpowered battle that pits the X-Men against their most dangerous foes. In a roleplaying game, the opposite might be true.

The great thing about a game, though, is that you can choose to focus on a single aspect of a story rather than trying to jam an entire saga into the game. You can hint at the larger story in color text, of course, but you can pick and choose the elements that best work in a game and, more importantly, fit the game you want to make. You get to highlight what works for your game and leave the rest of it to hide in the shadows.

FINDING THE FUSION

In the best games, the mechanics and the metaphor inform each other. They influence and support each other in intuitive ways at every level. If you get stuck on one aspect of developing the game, you can turn to the other for inspiration. As long as you respect both the mechanics and the metaphor, this works well.

When you're creating your own game, you can alter either aspect of a game to fit the other, but you need to make sure they always match up seamlessly. You don't always have the same freedom with games based on an existing story or property, but if the story can't bend, then push the mechanics toward it instead.

Either way, though, your finished game should never ring false. If it's a game about dueling wizards casting spells at each other across a fantastic and ever-changing landscape, then rules that factor in political intrigues at the emperor's high court will stab out at the players like a dagger. If the game's pitched as being a simple, light game for kids, but it takes twelve hours and a college education to complete, it's not going to fly.

The story tells the players what to expect from the game, and it's up to you as a designer to use every tool you have, including especially mechanics and metaphor, to deliver that to them in the best and clearest way you can. If you defy the players' expectations and give them something that doesn't mesh at all with what reasonable people would hope to find in the game, you wind up with players who are angry and confused. Those people might never come back to play your game again. There are just too many better options out there.

THE GAME'S THE THING

Any part of the game that fails to support the game and make it better—whether metaphor or mechanic—should be cut. It doesn't matter how enamored you might be of a particular mechanic or a clever bit of story. If it doesn't fit, let it go.

One of the best things about an idea is that it doesn't spoil if you leave it out. It has an infinite shelf life. You can always use it somewhere else later, in a project that suits it better than the one you're working on at the moment.

It's not always a matter of having to choose one thing over the other, of course. Sometimes, you need to find a balanced compromise, a happy medium between the two extremes. The best games don't favor abstract mechanics over story-rich metaphor, or vice versa. They mix them both up and blend them together into a recipe for fun.

Take a look at the territories in *Risk*, by way of example. The game is purportedly about trying to take over the world a nation at a time, but some nations are broken up into pieces, while others are grouped together for geographical convenience. It's set up this way because *Risk* works much better with 42 territories than trying to shoehorn in the nearly 200 nations we have in the real world. You'd need a magnifying glass to see some of the smaller places on the *Risk* board, and assigning proportional benefits to the more powerful nations would require you to shove cartfuls of playing pieces into them.

Similarly, any parts of the story that don't fit with the game can be jettisoned too, or at least ignored for the purposes of the game. Professor Plum may have a staggering backstory and a full character development arc that ends in a mind-shattering twist that would put *The Sixth Sense* to shame, but none of that matters in the game of *Clue*. If you want to tell those stories, either make the game specifically about them, or write a novel or short story instead.

In the end, it's your job to make every element of your game true to the game and to serve the entertainment of the people who will play it. If you can manage that, its pistons will hum like a choir.

Matt Forbeck *has designed collectible games (WildStorms, Marvel Heroes Battle Dice), board games (Dracula's Revenge), miniatures games (Silent Death: The Next Millennium), roleplaying games (Brave New World, The Lord of the Rings), and toys (Star Trek Mission Utility Belt, R.E.V.s), and has written novels, comic books, nonfiction, and computer game scripts and stories. For more about him and his work, visit Forbeck.com.*

Whose Game Is It Anyway?

by Mike Selinker

I'm not inclined to give you an introduction showing how cool I am. I'll let your judgment of that be based on how cool my friends are, as shown by their essays. But I will tell you how cool my name is. In real life, it's only moderately cool. "Mike" is a pretty dull name. But when it's printed on a game box, it's about as cool as it gets. That's happened to me several dozen times, and each time is just as thrilling as the first. You should want that. You should also know what having your name on a game means.

Board game designers, as a rule, are bright people. We honed that intelligence in the crucible of high school, where we might not have been the most expressive kids, or the most athletic, or the most popular. But we knew how to think, and craft, and process. For many of us, game design was the shop class we taught ourselves.

A consequence of that is that many of us are loners when it comes to design. Sports is most often a team activity, so those who focus on sports develop teamwork skills. Music is like that too, and so is dance. Science is flat out dangerous to do alone. There is a reason for finding collaborators in these activities.

Art, however, is not like that. Neither is writing. These are solitary activities because it is hard to imagine two people holding the same paintbrush, or typing the same word. When we seek out collaborators for these acts, it is usually a stacking process: first I pencil, then you ink. We do these things by ourselves, in caves of our own design. Home is where the brain is.

Game design feels like art, and it looks a lot like writing. It's miles of inspiration and frustration and anticipation. It doesn't give you the obvious hook for a partner. You can't run a pick-and-roll with a game design, because it's not at all apparent what the ball is.

But this is why it's so important to fight through that impulse and find someone to design with. There will be many games you design yourself, but if you cannot find it within yourself to share the process, then your game will be limited to the inspiration you can provide. Think about how many things in your life you share with others because of your own limitations. Don't imagine your game design is free from those.

I expect you know what your answer to this essay's titular question is. Or at least I have a pretty good guess what you want it to be. Your name's on the cover, so it's your game. That's a fine thing to believe. But it's more complicated than that. A game's identity is an amalgam of the people who breathe life into it. Let's take a look at the other people whose game it might be, and how your game should reflect those people's contributions.

IT'S YOUR CO-DESIGNER'S GAME

There is a chart that Shannon Appelcline put together in 2006 called "Six Degrees of Bruno Faidutti." Bruno, a Parisian designer, is one of the game industry's titans. He designed *Citadels*, a game that you should play often. And he is, in Shannon's words, "the Kevin Bacon of our gaming industry." Bruno thrives off his collaborators, which include American designer Alan R. Moon, German designer Michael Schacht, Italian designer Leo Colovini, and French designers Bruno Cathala, Serge Laget, and Ludovic Maublanc.

Shannon's chart is a giant hashiwokakero[5] puzzle, made up of a series of islands connected by bridges. On the islands are the names of dozens of designers, and on the bridges are the names of their collaboratively designed games. So on the bridge between the Brunos are *Boomtown, Igloo Igloo, Mission: Red Planet*, and *Queen's Necklace*.

I somehow ended up in the center of that chart. I'm on a cornflower blue island called "Hasbro," the company I worked at for a half dozen years. On the bridge between Bruno and me is the game *Key Largo*, which we co-designed with the late Paul Randles. I have another bridge to Larry Harris on which the 2004 revision of *Axis & Allies* and *Axis & Allies D-Day* appear, and yet another to James Ernest on which *Fightball, Gloria Mundi*, and *Pirates of the Spanish Main* appear.[6]

Axis & Allies is not anything like *Fightball*. One is a dramatic recreation of World War II, and the other is a futuristic basketball/rollerball mashup. But you can see my DNA in both of them. You can also see Larry's in *A&A*, and James's in *Fightball*, especially the grandiosity of the former and the *Button Men*-esque humor of the latter.

Those games are better for having that genetic conglomeration. I could have written a World War II game alone, and I could have written a basketball game alone. Nothing as good as those, though.

Finding your genetic matches can be quite the challenge, of course. Not everyone can design together. But you can't know until you try. Without collaborators, I'm not as good as I can be. That doesn't mean I can't make a game myself. But knowing that I can makes me comfortable with not doing it.

---

[5] Japanese for "build bridges."

[6] This chart was designed before we released the anthology board game *Stonehenge*, which caused Shannon some apoplexy. That game and its offshoots' authors were me, James, both Brunos, Serge, Richard Garfield, Richard Borg, Andy Looney, Klaus-Jürgen Wrede, and many others. It threatened to wreck the chart, so Shannon wisely disallowed it.

IT'S YOUR DEVELOPER'S GAME

Working on a *Magic: The Gathering* expansion can be a humbling process. Wizards of the Coast R&D puts together a team of up to five designers, who work together to brainstorm a hundred or more cards exploiting dozens of new game mechanics. Then, when they're done, they chuck it over a wall.

On the other side of the wall is the development team, comprised of four more R&D members and usually one member of the design team. The development team tears the design team's work apart, rebuilding it from the ground up. Then it goes to a rules manager for templating, and a continuity team for names and flavor text, and an editor for polishing. In all, up to 20 R&D staff members and writers might contribute to a single set of 350 cards.

This is not a place for the faint of heart. Attachment to your ideas can mean detachment from your *job*. But the point is not to make one person's ideas shine. The point is to make the game shine. At the end of this process, the game is as good as it can be.

You might not want to work in a smelting factory quite like that. But giving your game away to even one developer is a good thing. *Betrayal at House on the Hill* is a game that benefited from multiple voices. This haunted house game was innovative and well written when Bruce Glassco finished designing it in 1995. It became cohesive when Hasbro's Rob Daviau finished a redesign in 2001. It became streamlined and expansive when my team and I at Wizards finished a development pass in 2003. And it became far more polished when Bill McQuillan's team finished a second edition in 2010.

What scares designers about development is that they will no longer be able to see their own game. The good designers let it go. I had finished the design on the word game *Alpha Blitz*[7] when Paul Peterson cornered me in a hallway, pointed to a conference room, and whispered, "You'd better go in there. They're messing with your game." So I popped open the door, saw some surprised looks, and sat down to see what Jim Lin's team was doing. What they were doing was playing my game faster. Whereas my game was thoughtful and strategic, their evolving version was frenetic and heart-stopping. I had invented a new Scrabble, but they had invented a new Boggle. I watched the test, tipped my hat, and walked out of the room.

Now we had a dilemma. We had two very good, very similar games with very different play styles. Jim knew I wasn't just going to let my original game go, because I knew Scrabble players wouldn't pick up a game where they didn't

---

[7] *Alpha Blitz* is based on the "letter bank" puzzle, where you can use each letter any number of times, such as the letters in TORA making ROTATOR, or those in LENS making SENSELESS-NESS. The game was originally named *Letter Bombs*, since bomb cards took letters off the board. The brand team wisely objected to sending a game with that name through the postal system. In a naming meeting, this book's Kobold-in-Chief said, "You could call it something silly, like *Alpha Blitz*." I stood up and said, "Our work here is done," ignoring the anguished cries of "Wait, I didn't mean…" from Wolfgang.

get to use their entire brains. But I knew Jim wasn't going to let his game go, because he knew people who weren't as good at letter games needed more excitement. Rather than go to war, we hit upon the shockingly gentlemanly solution of putting both in the same box, one called "Alpha" and one called "Blitz." One Word Game of the Year award from Games magazine[8] later, we knew we had all done our jobs properly.

I rarely end up publishing two games for the price of one.[9] But if I know in advance that I will see someone else develop my game after I'm done with design, I feel liberated rather than constrained. If I don't like the results, I can say, "This needs to go back into design." That almost never happens, because my developers are really, really good.

IT'S YOUR PUBLISHER'S GAME

I walked into the Origins Game Fair intending to take one meeting all weekend. I found Larry, Bob, and Pete from Mayfair Games, and said, "I want to show you a game tomorrow morning at 11 am." They cleared their schedule, and met James and me for their first view of *Dust & Sin*, the game that would become *Lords of Vegas*. An hour later, they were ready to buy the game. Though I couldn't have known if they would like it, I knew that if they did like it, they would buy it. This was because of one thing only: I know their lines.

Lords of Vegas is a Eurostyle game with a major American twist. It looks and functions a bit like *Chinatown*, which looks and functions a bit like *Acquire*. If there's one thing every publisher of Eurogames wants, it's its own *Acquire*. Sid Sackson's game launched the German games revolution, massively influencing games such as *Modern Art* and *Manhattan* and many other fundaments of the current wave of board games. But *Lords of Vegas* has something none of those games have: four dozen dice. Eurogame manufacturers pride themselves on not having very much luck (other than card drawing) in their games, but American companies love dice. *Lords of Vegas* was a game designed for an American manufacturer of Eurogames. Say, Mayfair Games.

Lords of Vegas fit at Mayfair. *Button Men* fit at Cheapass Games. Despite Rob Daviau and Mike Gray's valiant efforts, *Betrayal at House on the Hill* did not fit at Hasbro's Avalon Hill division, which sat next to Parker Brothers and Milton Bradley. It was only when Avalon Hill was transferred to me at Wizards that

---

[8] It was my first of these, the second coming with the Cthulhu-themed word game *Unspeakable Words*, which shows the other end of the collaboration spectrum. The game came to me fully formed in the night after playing *Scrabble* and *Arkham Horror* at Monte and Sue Cook's house. *Unspeakable Words*, whose letters are valued by their numbers of angles, began life as *Hounds of Tindalos*, named for the Lovecraftian monsters who came through the corners of the walls. It later became *Bloodletters*, then *Cursed Words*, then its final title. I still need to do a word game calle *Bloodletters*. So if you're thinking of writing one: Back off, it's mine.

[9] Or five, in the case of *Stonehenge*.

it made sense. Even then, it was a struggle to get it published. A tile-based, roleplaying-style, component-heavy, semi-cooperative game with three rule books is not an easy sell in a corporate environment. But when it did come out, no one said, "Wow, I just can't understand why Wizards made that game." It was our game to make, even though it took ten years to get to us.

The brand identity of a publisher seems like a Rosetta stone to most designers. The question I get asked the most in seminars is "Who wants to publish this game?" The answers are obvious if you just take the time to understand who publishes what. If you're really good at this, you will start making educated guesses as to what a publisher might want to publish among things they don't currently publish. For example, some people were surprised when Fantasy Flight Games launched its Silver Line, made of board games for $20 and under. I wasn't. FFG published colossal $80 board games; when I worked on *Descent*'s *Quest Compendium*, they sent me the game and all its expansions in one box, nearly killing my postman. But there's only so many of those games a company can make without thinking, "Can we make some things that our customers can afford more easily?"

When you sell your game to a publisher, the aspects of that game that don't make sense for the publisher will start to fall away. Know that before you sign on the dotted line. If you can't see why a publisher would want to publish your game as is, it's probably because they don't. But they still might want it, and you still might like the results.

IT'S YOUR LICENSOR'S GAME

Merit: The Catholic Game was a Catholic dogma trivia game printed by the Educational Research Corporation in 1962. As noted by the tag "The Approved Game!" it was "printed with ecclesiastical approbation"—that is, approved by the Catholic Church itself. It's the only game I own with an "Extreme Unction" space.

Moving around the *Monopoly*-style board with tokens such as Christ the King and the Lady Madonna, *Merit* players draw questions from the Question Deck, such as "How many commandments are there?" or "Name the sorrowful mysteries of the rosary." Assuming a player can answer (per above, "Ten" or "Agony in the Garden, Scourging at the Pillar, Crowning of Thorns, Carrying of the Cross, Crucifixion, and Death of our Lord"), he or she moves forward the spaces indicated on the card. The player who returns home with 700 merits and six of the seven[10] sacraments wins.

The Educational Research Corporation's Edward J. Agnew received the Bishop of Spokane's approbation to print *Merit* on behalf of the Catholic Church. Agnew printed thousands of copies of the game. But the Church came out with its own release in 1962—a little thing called Vatican II. This

---

[10] Naturally you can't have both Matrimony and Holy Orders.

landmark convocation rebooted nearly everything about the practice of Catholicism, including the subjects of almost all of *Merit*'s trivia questions.[11] Even Extreme Unction was changed to the Sacrament of the Sick. Agnew's educational game now taught a dogma that the Church no longer espoused. And so the only copies I've ever seen are the four unpunched versions in my game closet.

Not every licensor is as tough on game designers as the Catholic Church, but it often seems that way. I've worked on a number of games based on other people's licenses: The Simpsons, Harry Potter, Spider-Man, Disney, and so forth. Licensors are not game publishers. Game publishers care about making great games. Licensors care about protecting their brands. The two concepts are related, but not identical.

Protecting a brand means fending off anyone who seeks to redefine it. While working on seven games for Marvel Comics properties, I came to understand that they were not likely to veto my game mechanics decisions. But if I put Spider-Man in a slightly incorrect suit, or made him say a line he would not, the wrath of Doctor Doom would come down. Marvel cares about what Spider-Man does, but as a rule it does not care what I make *you* do.

Protecting a brand also means making sure that the game is covered with expressions of brand identity. That usually means bedecking the box with logos. While creative director of licensed properties at Wizards, I once said in a meeting, "I'm not happy till my game looks like a race car." When pressed, I would say, "The more logos a game has, the worse it is."

But that's just chrome. The real impact is when a game changes for the worse because it and the brand conflict. Wizards made a great baseball trading card game called *MLB Showdown*, and another great soccer game called *Football Champions*. But when they tackled the other football, it became obvious to me that the gridiron game was just too complex for a TCG. Too much had to fall away: minor yardage plays, the offensive and defensive lines, and so on. As a football fan, I felt I couldn't resolve those inconsistencies, and I chose not to accept an offer to join the *NFL Showdown* team. I really wanted to work on an NFL game, but that one just wasn't for me.

When you get the opportunity to work on a great license, with a great licensor, the stars can align for some of the best work you will ever do. That will not happen every time. But in my case, it's happened enough.

IT'S YOUR GAME

What do you think of when you hear the words "Cheapass Games"? If you've never heard those words before, you think the games must be cheap. And they are. They're in white envelopes, and they don't come with dice or money or other fiddly bits. But if you have heard the words before, you not only think

---

[11] Same number of Commandments, though.

of those things, but you think of one other: the games are written and laid out by James Ernest.

James has a designer identity that permeates all the Cheapass Games. The games are arch in tone, a little DIY, and fairly bite size. You're not going to lose an entire day playing *Give Me the Brain* or *Kill Doctor Lucky*. But the part you do spend will be delightful, courtesy of the fine work by James.

He also produced some more expensive color games, and they were great too. But people didn't expect that from him. They wanted more of the white-envelope games, and so to do big-box games, he needed to break out of his carefully defined identity. That's where I came in. At that point, I made nothing but big-box games: *A&A*, *Risk Godstorm*, *Betrayal*, *D&D*'s 3rd Edition, and the like. That was my designer identity. And I wanted something James had. James had *cred*. His indie auteur approach made him a darling of the gaming elite, which sounded pretty good to me. He wanted to go big, and I wanted to go small. Our designer identities interleaved to make a team that people might expect anything from.

Designer identities can be constricting, but they're also good for business. Lisa Steenson's designs for Gut Bustin' Games are all deliciously low-rent: *Redneck Life*, *Trailer Park Wars!*, the garden gnome game *Oh Gnome You Don't!* If you like one, you'll like the others. You'll probably pick them up without even thinking about it.

If you have a designer identity, your game will be a reflection of it. Even if your name isn't on the box, people will figure it out. That's good. Don't let it restrict your creativity. Just own it.

IT'S EVERYBODY'S GAME

The credits on *Risk Godstorm* are these:

Game Design: Mike Selinker
Game Development: Richard Baker, Michael Donais, and Bill McQuillan
Based on the *Classic Game of RISK®* by Albert Lamorisse, and *RISK 2210 A.D.*™ by Craig Van Ness and Rob Daviau
Editing: Cal Moore
Cosmology: Brandon Bozzi, Eric Cagle, Brady Dommermuth, Skaff Elias, Chris Galvin, Brian Tinsman, and Teeuwynn Woodruff Game Design: Mike Selinker

---

And that's before we get to the artists and production people.

So is *Godstorm* my game? Well, sure it is. But it's also all those folks' game as well. We made it together. I had my hand on the tiller, but if Rich hadn't made the map and Mike hadn't made the cards and Craig and Rob hadn't adapted

Albert Lamorisse's[12] game to the futuristic 2210, *Godstorm* never happens. I know it, and the game says it.

The cheapest thing to give away is credit. If you're a credit hog, you will push people away from you. All my collaborators are listed next to my name wherever possible. When people tell you you've made a great game, you will do your team proud by saying, "No, we made a great game."

Mike Selinker *is president of the Seattle design studio Lone Shark Games. Among the games he has co-created are Pirates of the Spanish Main, Harrow, Lords of Vegas, Unspeakable Words, Yetisburg, Key Largo, and Gloria Mundi. Prior to forming Lone Shark, Mike was a creative director and inventor at Wizards of the Coast, where he helped launch games such as Axis & Allies Revised, D&D 3rd Edition, Risk Godstorm, AlphaBlitz, the Harry Potter Trading Card Game, the Marvel Super Heroes Adventure Game, and Betrayal at House on the Hill. His puzzles appear in The New York Times, Games, Wired, and other publications, plus in events and alternate reality games.*

---

[12] I'm sure if Lamorisse was alive, he'd appreciate what we did with his classic wargame. That is, if he wasn't too busy polishing his Best Screenplay Oscar and his Palme D'Or for *The Red Balloon*. And now you know who you want to be when you grow up.

Part 2
Design

In which we determine how our games will function, what they will look like, and whether or not they're any good at all.

How I Design a Game

by Andrew Looney

This book allows you to get inside the brains of over a dozen brilliant game designers. Yet I imagine that there's no brain in here that's built quite like Andy Looney's. Andy has let his brain be influenced by all manner of mind-altering substances—and by that I of course mean dice, cards, boards, and multicolored pyramids. He absorbs all, and returns to the world such wonders as Fluxx *and* Icehouse. *That's a brain you want to get inside. And you're in luck. Here he is, letting you in on how he designs a game.*

I'm not going describe how someone else should design a game—each artist has their own method of creating, often dictated by their particular situation. I'm simply going to explain my own process, a system I've figured out after decades of trial and error, in a way that will hopefully be of use, or at least of interest, to others.

The accompanying diagram is a flowchart of my process ("Figure 2-1. Flowchart of My Process" on page 35).

IT ALL BEGINS WITH AN IDEA

People often ask me where I get my ideas, and the truth is I really don't know—ideas just pop into my head. (If you aren't someone who just has random ideas, learning to design a game probably isn't your thing.)

THEME-DRIVEN VS. MECHANIC-DRIVEN

I have found that my games always begin with either a theme or a mechanism. For example, *Chrononauts* began with the thought, "I should do a card game about time travel!" From there it was a question of how to simulate the experience of time travel using playing cards. On the other hand, *Black ICE* started with the vision of memory game built on the shell-game-like structure of a row of three large opaque pyramids, each concealing a small pyramid. At first my working title was "Shell-House," since it was an *Icehouse* game inspired by a shell game. As the game developed, I realized that the perfect theme was computer hackers attempting to crack a password, which was represented by the hidden colors. But the theme fits the game so well, you'd think that's what I started with!

Sometimes it's very difficult to find a good theme for a mechanic-driven design. Pure abstract games certainly have their place, but I view that as a last resort. Even if a theme is very thin, it can help inspire the design in important ways, such as the choice of name. (Name design is often one of the most

Figure 2-1. Flowchart of My Process

difficult parts of game design.) Also, even if a theme starts out being too thin, the existence of a theme may inspire a new rule or two which makes the theme stronger. (That said, a pet peeve of mine is abstract games that purport to be about something but really aren't, so if a theme is too thin, don't try to force it.)

CARD GAME VS. BOARD GAME

Tabletop games are often split into the categories of card games and board games, but sometimes this distinction is strained. A lot of card games are basically board games with invisible gameboards. The timeline in *Chrononauts* is a gameboard made out of cards, and in *Aquarius* you build the gameboard as you go. Then again, a lot of Looney Pyramid games use no equipment other than the pyramids on a flat surface, but we call them board games. The problem here is the focus on the gameboard, which may or may not be an important element in a "board game." That's why I prefer the term "tabletop games" to refer to our products.

The difference is really that a card game uses nothing other than cards, while a board game uses playing pieces of other types, plus other stuff, like dice, cards, and usually a board.

REALITY CHECKS

Production issues should be considered early in the process. It's better to design in terms of what you can get manufactured than to attach yourself to the dream of a difficult to mass-produce design. (Trust me, I know.) Restrictions also help you focus your thinking, as anyone who's ever written a haiku or a 55-word short story will understand.

It's no good to create an awesome game that cannot feasibly be mass-produced. Similarly, designs based on licensed properties must be approached with caution, since you won't be able to publish your game if the license-holder turns you down.

Anyway, at this stage in my career, the process for me boils down into a pair of options: either a) card games that includes between 56 and 140 cards (ideally 100) and with no other elements that cannot be included in our standard Looney Labs card box, or b) board games that use Looney Pyramids. All of these are parameters I keep in mind as I create.

WRITE A DESIGN MEMO

I treat my new ideas as scientific discoveries. I keep a series of classic lab notebooks in which I jot down various ideas. (Long ago, as a young inventor, I read that it was a really good idea to maintain an inventor's journal, and I've often found that to be true.) When an idea seems particularly good, I'll write extensive notes on how I think it would work, and nothing helps separate the stupid ideas from the actual innovations like trying to write them down.

If you can put words to the idea and make sense of those words later on, you still may find that the idea wasn't as brilliant as you thought it was when you got out of bed at 3 a.m. to write it down because it seemed brilliant and you didn't want to forget it. Then again, it might just be that great idea you otherwise would have lost.

DEVELOP THE IDEA

Like explaining where ideas come from, this is another step that's really hard to describe. One analogy I like to use is to compare it to making a soup or a stew. You've got this simmering pot of stuff, and you're stirring it up, adding a little of this, a dash of that, tasting it as you go, trying to cook it up into something that *everyone* at the table will enjoy.

KNOW YOUR AUDIENCE

OK, first of all remember that you can't possibly make something that everyone will enjoy. Different tastes differ after all. No matter how yummy that veggie stew is, some folks just aren't going to want it, and you don't want to waste your time cooking it for them if they're just going to refuse it. So it's important to know your audience!

For me, the most important member of my target audience is myself. I figured out long ago that I'd have to be willing to play my own games ad nauseam if I were going to succeed in this business, and that I'd be miserable if the games I invent are not truly games I enjoy playing myself.

Anyway, I'm always collecting ideas and I've got lots of soups or stews going at once (Will it be a soup or a stew? Don't know yet!) and from time to time it becomes clear that something is ready and I serve it. Sometimes the stew will stay on the back burner for a long time, waiting for the right added ingredient to make it work, other times the soup will be ready so fast you'd think I used a mix.

(RE)BUILD A PROTOTYPE

Until the physical parts exist to try playing the game, it's just a bunch of ideas in a notebook. The main tools I use for building a prototype are the software packages called Photoshop and Illustrator (on a Macintosh, of course), whole sheet sticker paper, and the Image Search function on Google. I format card designs in nine-card sets which I can print onto a single sheet of unscored sticker paper. I cut these up by hand with scissors and stick them onto old cards. This makes for rather thick cards which can be a little difficult to shuffle, but it's a great way to make prototypes. When I'm just testing ideas I scrounge for clip art using Google Image Searches. (Of course it's understood that test art will be replaced with final art later, so it's not a problem to be using other people's images when it's only for testing purposes.) It's amazing what images will pop up when you type in various search words; that said, I sometimes cannot find exactly what I want and wind up doing a sketch of my own instead.

WRITE THE RULES

Maybe it's just because of all those years I spent working as a computer programmer, but I see many similarities between rules for a game and source code for a chunk of software. The rulesheet is like the program to be run by your players who together are the computer in this analogy. So the rulesheet, like the piece of software, must address every possible scenario problem and be as free as possible of both minor syntax errors and major crash possibilities.

It's important to write out the rules for the game you think you've designed even if it isn't complete. In fact, trying to write the rules down is a great way to show you the holes in your design.

THE SWEET SPOT

The Sweet Spot is a phase that begins as soon as I finish building a prototype (ideally complete with a draft of the rules).

The Sweet Spot is that blissful time when, as far as I know, my game works perfectly. As soon as someone actually tries playing it the problems may immediately become obvious, but until then I can enjoy the belief that this design will succeed where the previous versions failed.

Sometimes I'll be eager for someone to try out my new ideas ASAP, but usually I like to enjoy this moment in a game's life cycle, even to the point of reluctance to allow playtesting. But of course the Sweet Spot can only be prolonged so far.

PLAYTEST, PLAYTEST, PLAYTEST!

A successful game must be played over and over and over again before you can be sure that it works. One group of testers may have a great time because no one in that group is devious enough to try a game-breaking strategy. Or perhaps an unlikely combination of factors creates a rare situation that you won't realize ruins the game until you actually see it happen. So playtest as often as possible and with as many different groups and types of people as possible.

INNER CIRCLE

Setting aside solitaire tests and thought experiments, my playtesting begins with my inner circle of friends. These are my best gaming buddies, a group I've carefully cultivated over the years to be willing to try out every crazy idea

I've got and to give me their honest opinions. These are players who can take it in stride when I change the rules for the game they are playing as we play it—but I guess that's not surprising since I trained them all on *Fluxx*.

GET DEFENSIVE AND BROOD

Criticism can be difficult to handle, particularly when it's obvious to you as well as your players that your game design has blown up in your face. One good strategy is to think of it as a game you just lost and try to be a good sport about it. But that's not easy. It can be a big bummer. You find yourself wanting to explain why you thought it would go differently, and you may even want to blame the players for failing to have a good time. But you've got to listen carefully to the feedback and then say "Back to the drawing board!" Then retreat into your cave and ponder what went wrong until you come up with a new plan. Then either revise the prototype or build a totally new one and try again. Be sure to make plenty of notes in your inventor's notebook about what didn't work and what's new this time. Then enjoy being back in the Sweet Spot again!

THE FUN TEST

When do I know a game is "fun enough"? For me there's one simple test. When the game ends, do the losing players say "Let's play again!" or do they say "Well, that was interesting, what now?" If someone says "Let's play again" immediately after losing a game I designed, I usually say "Those are my three favorite words in the English language."

OUTER CIRCLE

After a new design passes the Fun Test with my Inner Circle, I start letting other friends try it out. Sometimes the design is functioning well by this stage and the main work is hammering out small problems; but other times the Outer Circle will point out problems the Inner Circle missed, and may even send me back to the Get Defensive and Brood stage.

RANDOM STRANGERS AND TRIAL BY RULESHEET

If a game design is successful, I'll move beyond testing with friends to see what random strangers think of it. And who are these random strangers? Well, ideally they are folks at gaming conventions or other venues where people who actually play games tend to congregate. Again, know your audience; actual random strangers may or may not even care for games, let alone yours.

At this point the focus shifts from making the game functional to making the rulesheet clear. As the design matures, so too will the written rules...but are they truly complete and adequately clear? To find out, I do something I call Trial by Rulesheet, which is to get a group to play a new game without any instruction from me. Instead, I instruct them to pretend they just got the game from the store and now must figure out how to play just from reading the rules. It's very difficult to resist the urge to answer their questions, but sometimes I just have to hold my tongue and smile. (Ideally I would have a testing room with a mirrored wall of one-way glass so I could watch them without being observed.) I watch them as they go through the steps of learning the game, and we discuss points of confusion afterwards, all the while looking for ways to make the rulesheet even more clear.

SIMPLIFY, SIMPLIFY, SIMPLIFY

To return to my soup/stew analogy, one thing you can't do very well when cooking is to take something out that you've added. So it can be with game rules. Sometimes it can be really obvious that a game has, shall we say, too much salt, and yet, it can be really difficult, emotionally, to axe an entire portion of a game that you've labored to create. Sometimes it can be literally unthinkable, in that the idea simply doesn't occur to you. And yet, trimming away that which doesn't work is one of the most important steps you can take. It may seem unthinkable to you that you could make the soup work without any chicken at all, since you originally planned it as a chicken soup; and yet, that could be the breakthrough that leads to your award-winning vegetable broth.

I was very inspired by the book *Good to Great* by Jim Collins, and one of the things I really took to heart in the book was the concept of the Stop Doing List. It can be very difficult to abandon a habit you've gotten into, but realizing that and dropping said habit can be the best decision ever.

I can also invoke the programming analogy here and talk about how simplifying game rules is like optimizing source code. A good software developer knows, for example, to look for redundant subroutines that can be combined into one, or for time-wasting blocks of code that can be sped up or deleted. By this same token, if you notice that your "software" is getting bogged down by a time-consuming process, make sure that section of the "program" is really important enough to be devoting that much processing time to. If not, simplify it so that it goes faster, or delete it altogether.

Basically, at every state I try to ask myself, "Is this element really working, and what happens if I get rid of it?"

PUBLISH!

The bottom row of my diagram is about the steps that happen after a game has gotten the green light for publication. But there's usually a long gap between the time when I feel a design is ready to publish and the Green Light Moment, and of course, I'm in the enviable position of knowing exactly who my publisher will be even if I can't predict when it will come to market. So even though my chart doesn't need a "Find Publisher" step, I suppose I should have added a box saying "Convince Team That This Game Should Get the Green Light."

I have a satchel filled with finished prototypes waiting for their day to go into production and until that day comes, all of those designs are technically still in the Playtest cycle. And every now and then I have a new idea for improving one of those unpublished prototypes, refining them even further, making them even more ready for their moment to shine.

When the light turns green, we proceed with commissioning final artwork, building out the finished card files using that artwork, designing the packaging and marketing materials, and doing all the other work it takes to publish a game. And inevitably, no matter how well designed the game, nor how complete the rulesheet, there will always be questions that come up after that glorious day when a game goes to the printer. But, hey, that's what internet FAQ files are for!

And that's how I design a game!

Andrew Looney *is the co-founder and Chief Creative Officer of the College Park, MD-based game company Looney Labs. He's best known for designing the many flavors of Fluxx, and for creating Looney Pyramids (a.k.a. Icehouse pieces). He is the designer of dozens of games for the pyramids, including Treehouse, IceTowers, Martian Chess, Martian Coasters, World War Five, IceDice, and Zark City. He's a Trekkie, a hippie, an Eagle Scout, and a former NASA engineer who once wrote software that flew on the Hubble Space Telescope.*

Design Intuitively

by Rob Daviau

If there's one person I know whose livelihood depends on people understanding his games right out of the box, it's Hasbro designer Rob Daviau. It is not uncommon for him to be presented with two simple beats ("It's Pixar's 'Cars' meets Operation!*"), and know that he has very little room for error in making his games intuitive. The cool thing about Rob is that when he tackles a more complex subject, such as* Risk: Black Ops *or* Heroscape, *you can see that intuitiveness beam through just as clearly.*

A few years back I was at MIT[13] and I had a room of about 25 ridiculously smart people at my disposal. So, like anyone, I tried a sadistic experiment. "Pair up," I said, "and choose a game that looks fun but you know nothing about." Eagerly they picked their games and returned to their seats, ready to open them and see what was in there.

"So the challenge is simple," I continued. "You and your teammate have five minutes to learn this game and present it to the rest of us.

"Oh, I've also removed all the rulebooks."

Take that, smart people.

But against every expectation I had, they did an amazing job. Now, granted, they spend most of their time inventing molecules or building cold fusion coffee makers, so they probably have a leg up on a lot of people. But the fact remains that people who'd never seen these games before could still intuit how to play them given nothing more than the bits, the box, and five minutes.[14]

This episode changed my entire outlook on game rules. I had, as you will, an epiphany:

> *Rules shouldn't explain a game;*
> *they should only confirm what the rest of the game tells you.*

That is, if your game makes intuitive sense from the moment players crack open the box, then you've done far more work toward people learning the game than you think.

Because tabletop games, unlike videogames, require every player to

---

[13] Many good stories start out with this phrase. Other good ways to start a story include "I was in a bar in Amsterdam," "It was about this time that the motorcycle lost control," "I don't remember actually getting the tattoo," and "An old man in robes sits down with your party and says 'I'm looking for some adventurers.'"

[14] You should try this sometime with a new game. Makes you see new games in a new way.

understand the entire game system to play. You need to understand not only the components, the goal, the rules, and the flow of play, but also how to assemble all these into a comprehensive strategy that will lead you to victory.[15]

We've all played games that make no sense at all, where every rule fights another and the pieces seem like an afterthought. Don't design one of those. Instead, design games that need the rulebook as little as possible.

If you are using the rulebook to fix an unintuitive game, you are making it very hard on your players to enjoy what you designed.

WHAT, EXACTLY, IS A GAME?

A while back I came up with my definition of what a game is, which is sort of a milestone for game designers.[16] We're going to use this definition to walk through different areas to focus on for intuitive design:

A game is an interactive mathematical system, made concrete, used to tell a story.

Just to clarify a bit:

- "interactive mathematical system" = mechanics and rules
- "made concrete" = pieces and graphics
- "story" = theme

Although all games have these three elements, the weighting of them varies greatly from game to game. Roleplaying games, for example, consist almost entirely of story with enough of a mathematical system to make the story work[17]; they can often play without pieces or graphics. Eurogames, on the other hand, are heavy on math systems, while the story is extraneous and the pieces are often reused from game to game. Abstract games ignore story entirely.[18] Miniatures games are all about the pieces. And so on. There is no magic weighting to these components. If you want to design a Eurogame, just know that your mathematical system is going to have a lot of weight, so pay particular attention to making that intuitive. Your audience will not mind a light theme or generic cubes and meeples. If you are designing a wargame, you're going to want elements more evenly weighted.

Let's take a look at how to make each component of this definition intuitive, so that players will enjoy your work without a struggle.

---

[15] And they should be fun, too. This may seem obvious, but I swear I've played some games that have missed this vital point and come across like graphics vomited onto a math problem.

[16] As is clinging to some design that you just love but everyone knows is awful.

[17] Honestly, you can ignore at least half the rules of any RPG system. RPGs don't have rules; they have *guidelines*. And 10 foot poles.

[18] Have you ever really felt like you're on a medieval battlefield while playing chess? Has it even crossed your mind?

THE JOYS OF AN INTUITIVE INTERACTIVE MATH SYSTEM

This is the nuts and bolts. The mechanics. The good stuff.

Every single game can be broken down into one ugly flowchart that defines everything players need to know about the order of play. I don't know anyone who actually makes this flowchart, even when designing, but I'll make an exception this time. Here is the flowchart to *Jenga*.[19]

Even if you don't flowchart your design, it still helps to think about it, so you can see exactly what it is you intend your players to learn and understand. If your flowchart has a whole side branch sprawling out to explain/control/balance one little part, then re-think that part. The more intuitive the mental flowchart, the easier your game will be to learn and the better it will be to play. The rules are usually the flowchart

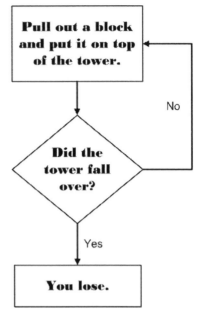

Figure 2-2. Flow Chart for *Jenga*

cleverly disguised as words, so you will know, once you get to rules, how intuitive your design is. If you can't explain something easily or you can't figure out what to explain first, you might want to go back and change the mechanics rather than spend time making the rules clearer. Rules are a poor patch for clunky design.

If you are reading this book[20], then probably you already can learn a game better than 99% of the people off the street. You read new rules and unconsciously figure out how this particular game fits your preconception of what a game is, based on hundreds of other games you've played in the past. But you're not designing games for you. You're designing for the other 99%.

So make your design as "clean" as possible, meaning all the mechanics are related and necessary. If your game requires players to roll a pool of dice and look for matches, then don't introduce a special case where players must roll

---

[19] I used to use *Candy Land* as an example of an easy flowchart only to discover that it isn't. It's not hard, mind you, but I looked like an idiot at a whiteboard getting the flowchart to *Candy Land* messed up.

[20] As if there were any other possibility.

one die and look for a number lower than four.[21] Likewise, don't make play go counter-clockwise, simply because you are bored of clockwise. Keep it simple and sensible: An elegant, easy-to-understand concept or mechanic that accomplishes 95% of what you want is much better than a clunky, obtuse mechanic that gets you 100%.

Similarly, if you have mechanics in there that come up extremely infrequently, try hard to close the loophole so you don't need the "patch." When I was finishing up work on *The Buffy the Vampire Slayer Game* in 2000 (most of the design is someone else's and I don't want to take credit for his brilliant work), we ran into the issue of Oz, who is sometimes human and sometimes a werewolf, possibly getting sired by a vampire. We had a full page of rules regarding werewolf vampires. The rules worked, had nice examples, and would be relevant so infrequently as to be useless. The entire page was changed to "Due to his werewolf blood, Oz cannot be sired." Is it more "realistic"? Probably not. More fun? Probably not, because werewolf vampires sound cool. Is it much easier to learn and play and teach new people? Yes, a thousand times yes.[22] Don't fall in love with a fringe element to your game.

Of course, no design *starts* clean and elegant and intuitive; what's important is that it ends up there. Some designers (like me) are sculptors: We cram everything we possibly can into our early game designs, and then, through testing, pare away everything that doesn't work. Other designers are more like painters, starting with a blank page and adding one mechanic at a time until they complete their design.

But keep in mind that even an elegant, intuitive system can be explained poorly, if you're not careful. For example, *Tigris & Euphrates*'s scoring system always gives new players pause. During the game, you earn four different colored cubes; your final score is your number of cubes in the color you have the *least* of. If you've never played *T&E*, then you probably stopped and reread that sentence; it certainly seems counterintuitive to focus on your weakest color for scoring. But if we change the wording to be "your final score equals the number of complete color sets you have," then suddenly, scoring makes a lot more sense. New players find it more obvious to group four colors into one set and think "that's one point," even though the scoring is exactly the same.

While playtesting your games, you will immediately notice which mechanics people forget or stumble over. If you find yourself constantly needing to

---

[21] In fact, high should be good, and low should be bad, unless you really can't do it any other way Yes, I would say—and have said—this to Larry Harris about *Axis & Allies*.

[22] Eight years later, I did the same thing to *Clue*. There used to be a whole block of rules about blocking people in a room, something that would be hard to do if you tried, let alone by accident. By changing the design to allow movement through other characters, I removed about two paragraphs of rules that shouldn't have been there in the first place.

remind players to roll a certain die at the end of their turns, for example, then you might want to find a different way to achieve the same effect in your design.

MAKING IT CONCRETE: GRAPHICS AND PIECES

Mechanics may be the wizard behind the curtain, but no one plays a flowchart. The flowchart is ever-present—an invisible, abstract set of what-nows and if-then statements floating in the players' minds. But the math must be transformed into something the players can see and touch and move: pieces, cards, dice. These parts dress up your math and make it real.

It's easy to overlook the physical chits and graphics, but you should put as much thought into these as you do the mechanics. The way a game looks and feels informs how the game will play, and serves as an unconscious reminder of the rules. Remember: the first thing players do when they open a new game is not pore over 50 pages of rules. No, the first thing they do is remove all the bits and pieces from the box, enjoying, even savoring, that magic moment of unknown about what they're going to play.

Physical pieces offer all sorts of opportunities to make your design as intuitive as possible:

- **Color:** If a player sees certain colors again and again, he will assume they go together in some way. If you give him four colors, and he knows it's a four-player game, then rightly or wrongly, he'll assume that each player takes pieces of that color. If this is not the case, you'll want to use another distinguishing characteristic—like shape—instead of color. And if your game uses colors in two different ways,[23] then use two different color systems. *Alhambra* makes the mistake of using the same colors two different ways. It's something players have to unlearn and gets in the way of just playing. Also, while we're at it: white means good and black means bad, if you have gold as money use yellow, and if you have wounds use red.

- **Form:** If it looks like a gun, it should shoot. If it looks like a boat, it should go on water. These are overly obvious examples, but consider how each of your pieces should look to best convey their function. If your boat moves three spaces, give it three oars. If it can attack twice, put two cannons on it. If it has a capacity of five cargo cubes, make sure five cargo cubes fit on it or it has a 5 printed on it.

- **Size:** Bigger means "more," "stronger," "elite," or "better." Small means the opposite.

- **Integration:** All the game pieces should work as a whole. If color plays a significant role in the game, then make sure the dice and card backs reflect the game's color scheme. Likewise, if your game includes round

---

[23] For example, one to track player identification, and another to track resources.

tokens, and your board has round spots on it, then players will naturally try to put the tokens on the spots.

- **Game board:** If your game has a board, look at it from many angles, not just right-side up. Does it still make sense when viewed upside down (as players sitting across the table will see it)? Likewise, we've all been trained that certain places on the board correspond to certain gameplay elements; e.g., a numerical track circumscribing the board means "scoring track." So if certain areas on the board relate to specific pieces or rules, mark them clearly, preferably with a ghosted (i.e., faded) symbol. And don't get complex with your symbols; if you're going to use one, make sure it still makes sense when faded on the board. And viewed upside-down. In low lighting.

- **Reference:** Don't clutter your board with useless information, but do make sure you use your real estate to provide reminders of key rule moments. If there's a space on the board that says "bank," and on the bank space is a "+3 coins" icon, then it's pretty intuitive what happens on that space. And while reference cards may seem redundant to you, to a new player they can be a godsend. Don't be ashamed to throw in reminders and reference cards.

The best way to test the physicality of your prototype is to do what I did at MIT: lay out the game without the rules and have someone try to figure out how to play. Listen in. Ask questions. Have your tester tell you what she has assumed about the gameplay. Chances are, she won't be able to figure it out entirely, but if you listen to the assumptions she makes, you'll learn much about what is (and is not) intuitive in your game.

TELL A STORY

Obviously story matters more to some games than others, but only designers of the most abstract games will ignore theme entirely. If you design Eurogames, theme often comes later—but still take the time to find one that makes the game instinctive.

A game's name and theme set the stage for the play more than you might think, and players can often experience mental whiplash on games that set certain expectations, only to veer in a different direction. The name *Galaxy Trucker* suggests that players will drive an interstellar truck, probably laden with cargo. Guess what? That's mostly what you do. *Race for the Galaxy*, on the other hand, suggests a racing game, or at least a contest to be the first to achieve something in the galaxy. In this case, not so much; the game is really about civilization building, which is a race. Sort of. Immediately, players have to unlearn their misconceptions before they can learn the game. It's still a very good game.

So if you call your game "Pirate Adventures: Mutiny on the High Seas," but it's actually a Eurogame about cargo loading and worker allocation, I'm taking a lot of time trying to figure out where my cannons and gold and plunder and buried treasure should be. But if you call it "Dockworkers and Cargo," I understand what I'm getting into. It's not nearly as exciting a name but, intuitively, I get it.[24] Great names should definitely be thematic and inspiring, yet capture exactly what the game is going to be about.

At the same time, be careful not to get so carried away with the theme that it creates obstacles for players learning the game. We all understand the concept of turns and rounds[25], or victory points and phases. So stick with the common terminology unless new words and phrases would make your game substantially easier to understand.

For example, if a scoring event occurs in your game at the end of four rounds, then you can write, "After four rounds, there is a scoring event to gain VPs." Predictable, but we all get it.

If your theme could bear "Four seasons make up a year, and there is a scoring event at the end of each year," then even better. It makes logical sense, and people instinctively expect something to occur after each winter passes.

But writing a rule like "There are four convocations, and after that there will be reckoning to gain Prestige points" is flirting, heavily, with confusion. Maybe it adds thematic drama, but explaining it requires so much unclear terminology that you'll only end up getting in the way of, you know, playing the game.

WHAT THE HELL DOES ALL THIS MEAN?

Designing games is not just about crafting rules that makes sense. It's about crafting an experience that makes so much sense that players become utterly immersed in the play.

Most people believe rules are the only thing standing between a designer's vision and the players' enjoyment. But the mechanics, the pieces, and the theme all work together to set the stage and emphasize what the player needs to absorb. Make all these components logical and cohesive—and intuitive— and you'll create a game that transcends the math and cardboard; a game where players aren't just cranking through a set of rules, but enjoying an experience, and telling a story. That game will have a life of its own, even before that rulebook is cracked open.

---

[24] "Dockworkers and Cargo" is actually an awful, awful name and would never, ever be bought by anyone who wants to have a fun time. But this is an article about design intuition, not naming games that sell.

[25] Although surprisingly, those two words are used interchangeably in different games. Can we create a convention right now? A player takes a turn. All the players taking one turn is a round. Who do I talk to about codifying this?

The views expressed are those of the author and do not necessarily represent the views of Hasbro, Inc.

Rob Daviau *started in the game industry by writing an article for Dragon magazine in 1998. This turned into a design job at Hasbro, where he has worked on all sorts of games for all ages. During this time he also designed or co-designed Risk 2210 A.D., Axis & Allies: Pacific, Risk Star Wars, Heroscape, and Risk Legacy.*

Come on in and Stay a While

Designing Gateway Games to Create New Gamers

by Lisa Steenson

Undoubtedly, you have a sour-faced 13-year-old niece whose iPod is jacked directly into her brain. If I get to pick one designer to try to convert that niece into a hardcore hobby gamer, I'm picking Gut Bustin' Games founder Lisa Steenson. Lisa has carved an identity with a set of hillbillyesque games that belies her sophisticated understanding of what makes games great. That she'll educate you with a Dale Earnhardt Jr.-branded can of Budweiser in her hand speaks volumes about how accessible she is. You can see it in her games, and in this essay about games that create lifelong gamers.

WHAT IS A GATEWAY GAME?

For the purpose of this essay, a gateway game will refer to a tabletop, traditional, or social game that can introduce non-gamers into the world of "game store games." Gateway games are found at game and hobby stores, and typically have a different style than the mass market games most Americans would point to when asked what a board game is. They usually differ from their better-known brethren in terms of strategy, complexity of play, or through their use of mechanics not familiar to those who grew up playing *Candy Land* and checkers.

GATEWAY FOR WHOM?

Gateway games are excellent for helping to bring significant others, non-gamer friends, family members, and people who are familiar only with the common offerings at the big box stores into the gamer fold, though hopefully not kicking and screaming. Some people simply are not game players and respecting that is important—plus, if these people are forced to play they can easily make the experience less fun for everyone involved. If you invite people who already enjoy playing some of the more common games in the *Sorry!-Scrabble-Monopoly-Uno* category, it will be easier to get them to learn and play a new game. However, the real beauty of a gateway game is that the rules should be easy enough for anyone to follow. When teaching new games, it is important not to overdo it: less is more! Introduce only a few new games so as not to overwhelm potential converts. If your new players come away wanting to play the game again or show a willingness to learn another new game, your evangelizing has been a success! Give yourself a high five and start planning your next game day.

There are three main reasons for playing board games:

1. **Socialization.** Board games bring people together in a way that is often lacking in the rest of our modern lives. In an increasingly individualized world more dependent on virtual friendships rather than physical ones every day, a fun activity that involves getting a bunch of people together to talk and compete can be pretty radical. It is this category that gateway games focus on the most.

2. **Challenge.** If you enjoy mentally pitting yourself against your friends (or even working together with them to solve a problem), board games are a great way to spend an evening. This is more likely a motivation of a gamer who has opted into the hobby.

3. **Hobby.** Game collecting and playing can also be a serious hobby for some. This may come about if a new gamer gets hooked and takes on gaming as a newly sparked interest. This is full commitment, and where you hope your gateway gamers will end up.

ATTRIBUTES OF A GATEWAY GAME

To be able to successfully develop a gateway game, we need to first consider what it is about these games that sets them apart from their kin. A few of these topics will also be considered in greater depth in the game development section. A gateway game has:

1. **Ease of learning.** A gateway game should be a breeze to start and teach. It should be possible to teach by demonstration, which should not take more than 10 minutes to introduce and get started. If the rules take a half hour to explain, you'll likely lose your window of opportunity as potential players start zoning out in a rules coma. This also applies to how the rules are laid out in the instructions—if the writing is confusing or poorly organized, you risk a game that either never gets off the ground or past the first round.

2. **Theme.** This is something catchy that draws players to the game and makes them want to pick it up. Overly "geeky" themes such as science fiction or fantasy might make casual gamers think twice about playing a game because it will feel too removed from their world. Themes that skew toward certain genders (wargames vs. dating games) or ages (stock trading vs. collecting baby animals) might limit your audience. A good gateway game's theme should appeal to a broad cross-section of people. Our *Redneck Life Board Game* has a fun, catchy theme that appeals to men and women, teens through grandparents, and is played by both self-proclaimed rednecks and sophisticates. Because of its theme, a wide spectrum of game players find it hitting their tables, and word of mouth keeps sales brisk.

3. **Lack of complexity.** A gateway game should not be overly complex. If we think of games as existing on a scale of 1 to 10, with 1 being something like War that relies only on the luck of the draw and 10 being, oh, a game that has its players recreating the Battle of the Bulge with miniature infantry units, a gateway game should fall somewhere in the 2 to 4 range. Complexity might also be variable. For instance, Gut Bustin' Games offers the basic version of *Oh Gnome You Don't!* as a 3 on that scale, and then as an advanced version that brings it up to a 4 for experienced gamers or players who have mastered the basic version. The number of action choices a player must consider; how cluttered the board is with components; and how much new information is presented each turn, whether as words or symbols on cards, on the board, or by some other means are all aspects that should be considered when it comes to game complexity. Keeping the level between 3 and 4 is a good target.

4. **Interactivity.** Being able to influence the actions or position of your fellow players lends to the social experience of playing a game, and helps avoid the so-called "multiplayer solitaire" feeling that some games can have. However, some players may feel threatened if there is too much backstabbing or conflict, leading to their having a bad experience and ruining the possibility of a replay. Avoid games that have an elimination mechanic unless the game is short, probably under 30 minutes, as the downsized players will become detached and uninterested.

5. **Luck.** Weaving a little luck into the game allows everyone to have some chance at winning or, at very least, finishing well. If a player is losing but has no chance to gain ground. It will take away from the experience. Luck can also provide the kind of small victories during play that help players to feel successful during the game even if they don't win.

6. **Duration.** A good gateway game should last somewhere between 45 and 90 minutes. A game that takes longer may lose newer players, while anything shorter than 30 minutes may leave its players feeling like their purchase was not a good value.

7. **Originality.** By using a new mechanic or theme, your game will stand out in the crowded game market. On the other hand, if your game makes its players say "Hey, this is really similar to such-and-such," you might just find them playing that game instead.

8. **Replay value.** In some ways, replayability can be seen as a players' feeling on the total value of your game. Good replay value comes from successfully balancing the above aspects within your game and will increase if the players have laughed and had fun, as they will want to recreate that experience both with the same group as well as wanting to introduce new players. However, if they were criticized for

lacking skill, made to feel stupid, felt ganged up on or awkward, sat around because they were eliminated, or found the theme boring, you won't get many takers the second time around. *Oh Gnome You Don't!* tends to finish with the players wanting to restart the game as they had fun with it and realize that they can play better next time by improving their strategy. There is some backstabbing, but not too much, and it is all in good fun.

DESIGNING A GATEWAY GAME

The first thing to consider in designing a game is concept. The inspiration for your game can come from many different sources; a theme, a new mechanic, a market segment, or even a tagline can all be germs from which your concept might spring. An excellent way to hone this concept is to ask yourself, "Who is this game for?" The more aligned all aspects of the game are to satisfying this question, the more successful your game will be. Remember that gateway games need to be fun, short, easy, and appeal to a wide segment of the population.

As you develop the concept of your game, weigh the importance in your game of the eight attributes listed above. One of the most important considerations should be complexity. There are many different things that can add to a game's complexity and each should be considered. For example, it might be good to limit the number of actions a player can take or the number of pieces out on the board. Even if the role of the bits out on the board is limited, just having to look at so many objects can scare away potential gamers. The same obviously goes for actions—I find it is much easier to get people started on a game if I can say something like, "On your turn there are only three things you can possibly do, so listen up." Three action choices per turn is a good number to shoot for in a gateway game, with each player choosing only one of the three. This helps the game move along more quickly and keeps learning fast and simple.

For instance, *Oh Gnome You Don't!* has four steps in a turn: roll, move, play a card, draw a card. Pretty easy. However, there are additional cards that let players "brawl" when they land on the same space as a competitor. This one added mechanic changes the dynamic of the game considerably and opens it up for greater strategy and more backstabbing. By adding the brawling feature to the game, some turns have a fifth step: roll, move, brawl, play, draw. For some players adding this fifth step can be too much, thus the option in the instructions to exclude or include the brawling.

Before we go too far, let's take a look into what made ancient board games successful in order to see if it might help with developing a gateway game. If you consider the history of our species, you'll find that almost every culture has developed games, as documented by amateur anthropologist Stewart Culin in a series of early 20th century books. if you look into what games tend to be distributed equally across cultures, one you'll definitely encounter everywhere is the race, or track, game. A race game is a game played by rolling a die (or throwing lots, or by using some other variation of this idea) and moving pieces along a track based on the roll. The first person to the end of the track wins. This kind of game relies wholly on luck, which seems at first to defeat the whole point of playing—why not just throw a die and make whoever rolled is highest the winner? Why play at all?

Part of the answer can be understood if we consider the work of behaviorist B.F. Skinner. He discovered that rats that were randomly rewarded with food for pushing a lever would sit all day mashing down on that lever, hoping for a treat. On the other hand, if the same treats came out at fixed intervals (for instance, for every third push on the lever), the rat would push it the requisite number of times, get the food, and leave. Animals, including us, are hard-wired to lust after random rewards. The other side of the answer is simple: luck levels the playing field. Even your four-year-old child can beat you in a game of *Candy Land*—which is why she will want to play it over chess. It is a game that fits its niche perfectly because everyone is equally able to win. If you consider the purpose of gateway games, you can see that the addition of luck can be an important one: players who haven't done much gaming at all stand a pretty good chance of coming away a winner. And if they win, they'll be more likely to play the game again. And again!

Limiting the complexity of your game doesn't have to mean that once players master it they will inevitably stop playing. There are many things that you can do to avoid losing players who have mastered the game. Dividing the instructions into two or three levels of complexity is one way to provide different groups with more options. Add advanced elements so that even players who have played a ton of times will have something to keep them playing. Some ideas for including different levels of play in the same box may include:

1. A variety of dice.
2. Additional cards to add into the game. More intricate cards might be produced in a certain color to be brought out for later, more advanced play.
3. A new mechanic, such as *Oh Gnome You Don't!*'s optional brawling mechanic.
4. An additional means of scoring. There might be, for instance, another scoring variable that could be withheld until players have mastered the basic game rules.

The same ideas hold for developing expansions for your game. For instance, *Redneck Life* has an expansion that provides a greater variety of rigs and homes, all new charts, different redneck name choices for the players, and 50 more draw pile cards. Expansions not only increase replay value, but can provide you with a way to keep the initial cost of the game lower, allowing you to then sell the expansion or additional components for half again the amount of the base game. And since the initial game was easy to learn, you'll have players ready to add a little something extra to expand the experience.

One thing we have not yet discussed is the visual presentation of the game, including its box artwork, board, and components. While we've all been told not to judge a book by its cover, I'd bet that every one of us has picked up a book solely because it had great design. And why not? If a beginning gamer wandered into a store looking for something fun to play with his friends and family, he would be far more likely to pick up a game that looks cool, colorful, and fun. This will make it an easier sell both for purchasers *and* players. Gamers like to have components in front of them to touch—cards, wooden pieces, money, blocks, little plastic trinkets, anything that gives them a physical connection to the game. Similarly, the name of your game is critical. It needs to elicit a response that will intrigue the shopper enough that they want to pick it up and learn more. Once the box is in her hands, the artwork and back of the box should do the rest, helping to draw the buyer into wanting to play. The price point will have to be considered after reading the back of the box and the shopper will be subconsciously weighing the game in their hands to feel if there is value inside. If the theme, artwork, description, heft factor, and pricing come together,s you have a sale…and hopefully, once it has been played, word of mouth that will lead to more sales!

A gateway game does not have to include all of the attributes mentioned in this essay, but the more you can implement into your game, the better its chances for success. Gamers want to open others' eyes and minds to new games, breeding a new generation of players. If their friends and family have a great experience, they will be eager for your next offering. Then you've made them into gamers.

Lisa Steenson *is the Grand Pooh-Bah of Gut Bustin' Games in Battle Ground, Washington. She designed its board games Redneck Life, its expansion Bustin' a Gut, Trailer Park Wars!, and Oh Gnome You Don't! Her games are sold in 2,500 game, hobby, gift, sporting goods, farm supply, and drug stores, as well as on Walmart.com, Target.com, and ToysRUs. com. Lisa's convention staff includes her three daughters, Raina, Jill and Lauren, who are known as "The Gut Bustin' Gals." Her website is www.GutBustinGames.com.*

The Most Beautiful Game Mechanics

by Mike Selinker

I write a column called The Most Beautiful Things (http://selinker.livejournal. com), in which I discuss the things that are more beautiful, more elegant, and more fulfilling than anything else of their type. This is a gamer's version of that column, dedicated to the best game mechanics found in the card and board games I've played. These are the mechanics that only morality and respect for the legal system stops designers from stealing. Well, maybe only respect for the legal system.

What makes a game beautiful? Not sales, that's for sure. Not awards, as if those mean anything at all. I won't even dignify the suggestion that reviews are involved. No, those strawmen aren't what people think of when they think of beautiful games. They think of pretty components and social interaction, and, even if they don't put their finger on it, they think of game mechanics.

Beauty is in any of the eleven eyes of the beholder, of course. For me the test is "does this rule make me want to play this game right now?" *Scrabble*, as good as it is, doesn't have any of those rules. It's just a process, dependent solely on the ability of you and your opponents. But a beautiful mechanic makes you talk of it like it played the game for you. It's a part of your experience—a vector for your imagination. Understanding what makes these beautiful will let you craft mechanics that are their equal, but only if you work at it. This group of ten mechanics, in chronological order, is the bar. Aim for clearing it.

KINGMAKER'S NOBLESSE OBLIGE

In the 1974 Avalon Hill game *Kingmaker*, designer Andrew McNeil wanted to simulate everyone and everything central to the War of the Roses. This was a tall order indeed. A key problem he faced was that certain nobles in the game were more historically significant—and thus more powerful—than others. A lesser designer might have costed these nobles as more expensive, but McNeil took a different path. Over the course of the game, various events will occur: piracy, bad weather, plagues, and the like. If you have a powerful noble, these events might sweep him away. For example, one of the Peasant Revolt cards says "Neville to Raby, Scrope to Masham, Roos to Helmsley, Mowbray to Wressle, Archbishop of York to York, Marshal to Wakefield." If you bet your money on those nobles, you suddenly wonder where they've gone during your pivotal storming of Nottingham Castle. *Kingmaker* figured out that players are attracted to shiny objects: A transcendent noble such as Percy is one of the most useful nobles in the game—if he's ever around for you to use him. But when he's off in the hinterlands repelling the Scots, meeting in a religious diet, or dying of the plague, you will regret depending on him. So all nobles are equal, even though some are created more equal than others.

BATTLETECH'S HEAT

I'm a fan of mechanics that force players to make hard choices. If you do only one thing well, and you can do it all the time, you never make any choices. In FASA's 1984 giant-robot game *BattleTech*, your BattleMech can do only one thing well: blow stuff up. But if you fire everything you can in a turn, your "heat level" goes up. In addition to cooking your pilot, overheating your 'Mech will fuse your weapon systems, lock up your legs, and disable your targeting screen. You'll be a sitting duck. But of course, if you *don't* fire your weapons, you'll be just as dead. Heat made the game strategic. It also translated well to other versions beyond the tabletop game. Most notably, the *BattleTech* pods (giant videogame cabinets you could climb inside) flash disorienting lights when you overheat, and invariably this will be followed by your 'Mech exploding into a million pieces. And yet you still will unload everything the next time a Blackhawk goes zipping around your lumbering Atlas. A good rule can only teach you how to use it. The rest is up to you.

SET'S SET-MAKING

There are 81 cards in geneticist Marsha Falco's 1990 classic *Set*, and they are the only 81 that can ever exist for it. Cards have four features: number (one, two, or three), color (red, green, or purple), shading (solid, striped, or open), and symbol (diamond, squiggle, or oval). Using that information, Falco built a game that is about staring at a set of cards until you can find a "set." That's a group of three cards for which each of those four features is either all the same or all different. That means that for every two cards in the game, there is exactly one that makes a set with them. So if you have 2-red-solid-oval and 3-red-solid-diamond, you must find the 1-red-solid-squiggle at once. But you don't just have those two. You have ten other cards, and the sheer sensory input can be overwhelming. And you have a bunch of other players all trying to finding that set in real time. All of this with just diamonds, ovals, and squiggles.

MAGIC'S CARD TAPPING

One of the most interesting (and patentable) dynamics of Wizards of the Coast's 1993 sensation *Magic: The Gathering* was Richard Garfield's concept that a trading card has an "on" and an "off" state, symbolized by the turning of the card 90 degrees clockwise. The fact that it's called "tapping," etymologically symbolizing the draining of energy from the card, is a nice bonus as well. I can't remember ever seeing that conceit in a card game before that; it was occasionally reserved for much more physical components, such as submerged submarines lying on their side in *Axis & Allies*. However, the state of "tappedness" conveyed hundreds of pieces of game information. Tapped cards couldn't attack or use powers that required tapping; untapped cards couldn't untap, an action that triggers all sorts of other actions. What really made tapping sing was the instant visual summary of a game in progress. You could tell from ten feet overhead which player had a lot of resources to attack with, and which didn't. That made it a lot more visually appealing on the occasions when the game appeared on ESPN.

BATTLE CATTLE'S COW TIPPING RULE

In Wingnut Games's amusing 1996 miniatures game *Battle Cattle*, you control giant armored cows that fire missiles at each other. The rule that blew me off my chair was, of all things, the Tipping Defense Number (TDN). Each cow has a Tipping Defense Number that correlates with its weight. A very heavy cow has a low TDN (3 or 4), while a very light cow has a high TDN (10 or 11). When someone rams a cow into your cow, you have to roll above your cow's TDN to have it stay standing. However, after your cow is tipped, you have to roll below your cow's TDN to have it get back up. One stat covers weight, gainliness, and coordination. Choosing a cow with a high TDN makes it likely it will go down, but likely you'll get it back up again before anything bad happens. Choosing a low TDN makes your cow the Rock of Gibraltar, but getting your cow back up again is nigh impossible. That kind of symmetry is just amazing. And it occurs in a game about cows.

XXXENOPHILE'S POPPING

In James Ernest's mildly pornographic 1996 trading card game *xXxenophile*, based on the not-at-all-mildly pornographic Phil Foglio comic book of the same name, some cards caused your opponent to lose an item of clothing. That's pretty ballsy. But what was even cooler was that each card border sported a set of numbered symbols. Each turn, you could spin a card 180 degrees, and if the symbols along the edges of adjacent cards matched in shape, the one with the lower number of those symbols "pops" off the board. If the two sets of matching symbols also matched in number, they both popped. If you had two edges that matched symbols of two adjacent cards, you popped the cards on both sides. What I love about the popping rule is that at heart, it's a straight numerical comparison based on like statistics, as if it were "Compare attack scores, and higher wins." But it's so much prettier and so much more active than that, with the spinning and the color matching and the cards leaping off the board. The system was revolutionary, both literally and figuratively. (Side note: The term "popping" also had a sexual connotation in the game, which rather hastily disappeared when these mechanics got ported to the G-rated game *Girl Genius: The Works*.)

BOHNANZA'S HAND ORDER RULE

If farming beans doesn't sound exciting to you, you obviously haven't played Uwe Rosenberg's 1997 German card game *Bohnanza*. What makes it great is a mandate to keep your cards in the order in which you drew them. At the start of each turn, you must plant the first one or two bean cards from your hand into your precious two bean fields, each of which can contain only one variety of bean. Then you draw two cards, which you must plant or trade. Since you have only two bean fields, those two cards will overrun any beans of different varieties. So you have to get rid of unwanted beans by trading them, and other cards from your hand, before your fixed hand order makes you plant them. If you can maximize your harvests before you have to tear them up, you will be crowned the king of beans. All this pressure and interaction is caused by *stopping* you from doing the most natural thing: rearranging your cards in hand.

MISSISSIPPI QUEEN'S PADDLEWHEELS

In Werner Hodel's 1997 game *Mississippi Queen*, each player helms a paddlewheeler down the Mighty Mississip, picking up Southern belles for delivery to the delta. A boat contains two six-faceted paddlewheels: one controls speed and the other coal. You start out moving at speed 1, and you can rotate the speed wheel up or down 1 each turn. If that's not good enough for you, you can burn off coal to accelerate or decelerate some more. Speed is used to move or turn that number of spaces, no more and no less. However, you have a problem. Since you must move as much as your speed indicates, breaknecking down the river can cause you to not stop in time to avoid crashing into a riverbank or an island. This process is complicated by the fact that *you have no idea where you're going*. When a player crosses a line on a tile, that player places the subsequent river tile in whichever direction he or she wants. Run out of river and you're gator bait. Glory be.

TIME'S UP!'S COMMUNICATION BREAKDOWN

In 1999's *Time's Up!*, Peter Sarrett codified the antiquated game *Celebrities* into its modern form. The goal is to have your partner(s) guess celebrity names that you've drawn from a pool of cards, and each one does so based on clues you provide during a short burst of time. If that were all there were to the game, it would not be a party classic. What makes it work is its limitation of communication over time. *Time's Up!* requires everyone to remember everything that happened during round 1 of the game, when a dozen or more celebs were guessed. That's because in round 2, you have to guess the same celebrities, except that for each, you can say only *one word*. So if you originally clued Brad Pitt as "that actor who was in *Ocean's Eleven* with George Clooney," for the next round you might just say "*Ocean's*" or "Clooney." One word might sound tough, but it's a walk in the park compared to round 3, where you must clue the same celebrities with *no words at all*. Maybe you use your hand to indicate a big chin—even though George Clooney's not even the guy you're cluing. Maybe your partner will get it. Maybe.

DOMINION'S CONSTANT SHUFFLING

For at least a decade, game designers theorized the concept of a standalone deckbuilding game, where players made their own decks from a fixed set. But nobody made one. Something was missing from the concept and held it back. Donald X. Vaccarino realized that the key was to build the deck over the course of the game. Still, even that wouldn't have made 2008's *Dominion* work. The real innovation was to get the players to dump their hands at the ends of their turns. You start with a mere ten cards in your deck, draw the first five, play some, and discard the rest. On the next turn, you draw the next five, play some, discard the rest, and are *out of cards*. So you're shuffling within the first few minutes of the game, and a heck of a lot thereafter. This means that cards that you buy will show up in your hand not too long thereafter. Your deck builds because you're cycling through it at rocket speed. That's why *Dominion* is the best game of the last decade

Mike Selinker *is president of the Seattle design studio Lone Shark Games. Among the games he has co-created are Pirates of the Spanish Main, Harrow, Lords of Vegas, Unspeakable Words, Yetisburg, Key Largo, and Gloria Mundi. Prior to forming Lone Shark, Mike was a creative director and inventor at Wizards of the Coast, where he helped launch games like Axis & Allies Revised, D&D 3rd edition, Risk Godstorm, AlphaBlitz, the Harry Potter Trading Card Game, the Marvel Super Heroes Adventure Game, and Betrayal at House on the Hill. His puzzles appear in The New York Times, Games, Wired, and other publications, plus in events and alternate reality games.*

Strategy Is Luck

by James Ernest

James returns with a pair of complementary essays that deal with chaos and luck. The first examines a game design question you've probably asked yourself a hundred times: "Where should my game fall on the strategy/luck axis?" There's even a slider on the back of your game box—the one that has STRATEGY on one side and LUCK on the other—that will tell you in no uncertain terms that you must answer that question. But those words are no more opposites than clowns and ice cream. You can, and will, have both in most games you make. Here, James tells us why.

STRATEGY IS LUCK.

Do I have your attention?

Okay, let's be clear. I'm not saying that strategy is luck, even though that's the title of the article. My actual thesis here is that "strategy" and "skill" are different, and the main difference between them is that strategy has a luck component, while "skill" doesn't. Understanding the roles of luck, strategy, and skill will help you design better games.

Here are the terms.

- **Luck:** In games, "luck" is not necessarily "good luck" or "bad luck." It's just something beyond your control. It's a fork in the road, a random choice that might help you or hurt you. It might be a die roll, a card flip, or the actions of other players.
- **Strategy:** "Strategy" is the act of making plans and decisions during the game, given limited information.
- **Skill:** "Skill" is an aptitude for the game that you bring from the outside. Specifically, skill allows you to know the correct choice in a given situation.

Games usually have all three of these elements. And, not as obviously, the proportions can vary from one player to the next.

When a player is new to blackjack, he faces many choices that he has never considered before. Shall I hit or stand on a 16? What extra information can I bring to bear on this? Are previous hands important? What about the dealer's exposed card?

This kind of decision making is part of what makes games fun. Players like to improvise, try new solutions, and find the limits of the game space. As Raph Koster points out in his book *A Theory of Fun for Game Design*, a player will have fun as long as he comprehends his options, yet doesn't always know the right solution. If a player doesn't understand what's happening, he gets frustrated. If he knows it all (or thinks he does), he gets bored. The sweet spot called "fun" exists between these two extremes.

To play blackjack well takes more than on-the-fly decision making. It takes skill. Beyond a very basic level, that isn't really something you can develop while you play. You will need charts, computers, help, and practice. As you learn the game, your strategic play is replaced with skill.

Basic strategy says that you should hit your 16 whenever the dealer's upcard is greater than 6. Every time. If this is your playbook, this choice has become a rote decision for you. When you learn to count cards, you can fine-tune this decision, but even then it's still a matter of routine. Given the current count, or whatever else you know about the deck, there is no question about whether you should hit or stand on this hand. And because you can play perfectly, this decision is no longer fun. The only "fun" that is left is the thrill of beating the casino. And good luck with that. Hint: It requires a false mustache.

I think most people would say that "strategy" is what you are using when you play perfect blackjack. I think that is a case of one word meaning two things. I prefer to think of the educated guesswork that you start with as "strategy," and the robotic execution of known decisions as "skill."

Blackjack is, for the purposes of this discussion, a solved game. But in games where a perfect solution is not known, "educated guesswork" is the only available mode of play. For example, given a random setup in *Settlers of Catan*, there is probably a single perfect opening play. But there is no book to learn it from, no perfect play table to consult, and so players must use strategy.

Are all strategic decisions correct? By my definition, the answer is no. After you eliminate all the moves that you know (or think) to be wrong, any choice that you make between the remaining moves becomes a matter of luck.

Expert players struggle to minimize the luck element by knowing the optimal move in every situation. Over time, they replace guesswork with skill. Until that point, making the right strategic decision relies on guessing.

TIC-TAC-TOE

You're five, and you're playing tic-tac-toe. You make your moves randomly, and so does your opponent, because he's a good father. For you, tic-tac-toe is a game of pure luck. You are trying to make the right random decisions in a world of random decisions, resulting in the occasional win, and a fun-filled tour of the game space.

After a while, your dad starts winning, because he thinks it's time you learned a valuable lesson: that he was letting you win. He teaches you to spot threats, and block his XX with your O. Then he teaches you to spot opportunities to make your own threats. And all of this is wonderful until he gets to the punch line, which is that tic-tac-toe is not much of a game.

For your dad, this is true. It's not a game at all; it's an exercise. It is a solved problem. He can always win as the first player, always win or tie as the second. And this is what he wants to teach you. He also has something to say about Santa Claus.

Is he still a good father? Sure. In his "bring up my child" game, he figures his best move is to teach you about strategy, by teaching you the solution to tic-tac-toe. And while he's doing this, he also teaches you about chess.

Chess is a game of "strategy," he tells you, "much better than tic-tac-toe because it requires thought. It can't be solved." And while it's true that you wouldn't really call tic-tac-toe a strategy game anymore, there is no structural difference between the two. It's just a matter of scale. They are both perfect-knowledge turn-based abstract strategy games in which players choose from a finite list of moves on each turn. So how are they fundamentally different kinds of game?

The big difference is scope, not form. The games differ only in that no player has the aptitude to beat chess with the certainty that a player can beat tic-tac-toe. There are more different chess games than there are atoms in the universe. Way more. On the other hand, the number of different tic-tac-toe games is about 30. (Okay, it's actually 26,830, but it sure feels like 30.)

The adult chess player is exactly like the juvenile tic-tac-toe player. He is making his best guess from among several moves, and not always making the best choice. If a player can't identify the optimal move among several; indeed, if no one can conclusively prove the optimal move, then how is this distinct from guessing? And if your guess is equally likely to be wrong or right, how is that not luck?

As it turns out, chess is partway solved. There are a lot of opening moves to learn (akin to "put X in the center square"), which means that expert chess players can go through of memorized moves before they have to start improvising. Bobby Fischer hated this aspect of chess. He found the modern state of chess, where memorization trumps strategy, to be "uncreative." So he popularized a form of chess that obliterates opening move memorization by randomizing the initial setup. It's called *Chess960* for the 960 different legal ways to set up. But really, it should be called "Chess959," because who wants to play setup number 1?

"Creativity," as Fischer suggests, is what makes games fun to play. Learning perfect strategy does not make a game more fun; it just makes it more likely that you will win. And while it's easy to get hooked by the notion that "winning equals fun," you can make a lot more money as an accountant than as a professional blackjack player, and you don't have to wear a false mustache.

And yes, there are more nuanced layers of skill and strategy than I'm talking about here: to make a strategic move in chess, you bring a general "skill at playing chess" to each decision point. So general skill still has bearing on strategy in that you can more easily prune out moves that are clearly not the best. But among the moves you have left, you're still guessing.

HOW DOES THIS HELP US DESIGN GAMES?

It's easy to get confused in the process of designing a game. If you want to make a strategy game, you want it to have "interesting decisions." Do you want those decisions to be hard? Probably not. Do you want them to have obvious solutions? Probably not. Well, is there a third choice? How can they be simple and still not obvious?

In some games, the "simple but not obvious" choices are constructed using randomizers. For example, you must bet on a number, then roll two dice. If your number comes up, you win. If not, you lose. Voilà, craps has decisions that are simple but not obvious. But it's not a strategy game.

One thing that makes a decision obvious is repetition. The first time you see a particular situation, you don't know what to do. The tenth time, it's an easy decision. You'll start doing the same thing even if you have a bad habit of doing it wrong. Watch a new player learn blackjack, and he will quickly fall into patterns, including bad ones. But playing by a chart, even a bad one, isn't that much fun.

What about a game where the decisions are simple but not familiar? This is the right solution. To work, this game must have a broad range of game states, such that players often find themselves in new places, yet always feel equipped to understand their options. And in these situations, there is rarely a single obvious choice. This is a tough design challenge, but it's at least good to know that you are aiming for it.

Poker is a game like this. In Texas hold 'em, the variables of hand, board, and position make for thousands of basic game states. And in each state, the player's options are tightly limited. Yet, in each case, given other information such as play history and personal style, the optimal move is difficult to find. Do you fold aces? Sometimes. Do you push with nothing? Sometimes.

Longer games give you more opportunity to build meaningfully different, but simple, situations. In *Monopoly*, a player's choices can be simple and not obvious. *Monopoly* doesn't give you much choice in where to move, so your main decisions revolve around how to spend your money. At different stages of the game, nearly every variable can change: how much money you have, how much property is already owned, where other players stand, and so on. And these game states never repeat from game to game, so there can be no lookup table telling you what to do in a given scenario.

As long as players can continue to encounter meaningfully different game states, they will enjoy making decisions on the fly. If they decide that they have seen everything your game has to offer, this is the moment when it transforms from chess to tic-tac-toe.

To build the concept of "strategy is luck" into your game, give players the chance to be creative. Give them new situations with clearly defined choices. Don't require them to memorize tables, because this is not what they want to do. Give them situations where they are clear on their options but not clear on the right move. Then they will really have fun.

Let's Make It Interesting

Designing Gambling Games

by James Ernest

At first blush, gambling games might seem outside this book's scope. They do have cards and dice and spinners and charts and people sitting around tables lamenting their fortunes. What they don't have is a perception of fairness for all participants. And for some designers, that's non-negotiable. "Why would I play that?," you think as you look at the Mega Millions jackpot. And then, as it rolls up its eighth digit, you do. You should know why, and James will tell you, for a fraction of the cost. Step right up.

"Let's make it interesting." It means "Let's gamble." It's a promise to take an activity that was, by implication, not interesting, and bet on it. How does gambling make simple games interesting, and how does a game designer set about creating a new gambling game?

First, let's talk about why gambling is fun.

I don't watch football. I don't care for it. I have no emotion invested in my local sports franchise and frankly, the way most major sports figures change teams, I can't imagine how anyone does.

But if I'm watching a game and I arbitrarily pick someone to root for, I can start caring about the game. My team gets ahead, and it falls behind. I celebrate their successes. I feel their losses. And there's no surer way to get involved than to make a bet.

Do I have any impact on who wins? Of course not. But I still care. I'm engaged by the story of my wager, which becomes the story of my team. The fact that there is no "strategy" in winning this bet doesn't even enter into my thoughts. I don't need that kind of stress. I just want to be entertained.

I could probably rationalize my choice, as many people do. I could argue that I made a bet based on some criteria that will prove that my team was more likely to win. But most people don't think like that. Players who root for one team over another are usually doing it for emotional reasons. They bet on their home team.

Now, let's take that to the casino.

When you walk into a casino with a game designer, he can tell you how every game is a sucker bet. You can't beat any game but blackjack (and that's really hard). So you shouldn't try. If you must gamble, play craps. But only bet the pass line, and take the full odds. And whatever you do, never give a dollar to the keno runner. She will never bring it back.

Sure. This is the perspective of a rational person. So, does that mean that the casino industry is in trouble? No. Okay, so does it mean that gamblers are irrational? No again. Game designer types like to convince themselves that gamblers are deluded and stupid, but it just isn't true.

If you quiz real live gamblers about the risks they are taking, they are very up-front with you. They know that the house has an edge. They know they will probably lose. Their strategies are designed to make their bankroll last as long as possible, not to actually make money. If they wanted to make money, they would go to work.

They gamble because they enjoy the experience. Sitting on the edge of your seat watching your bankroll rocket up and down gives you the same thrill as watching your home team running back and forth on the field. Yes, you could win. But it's not likely. And as it is with the home team, you're happy to bet on yourself, even when the odds are against you.

When you walk through a casino with a gambler, she will tell you stories about big jackpots she's won, the slots with the best bonus games, and why she never plays roulette because of that time in Reno. She won't tell you if she's up or down for her career, because she really doesn't know. Not because she's a poor record keeper. Because she really doesn't care.

I'm going to say that again. She really doesn't care.

You're probably a game designer, and like most game designers you have some grasp of probability and statistics. You prefer to play games with strategy, because you like actually playing a game instead of watching it happen. There is no way that you would bet on a game you are likely to lose. So you just don't like gambling, and you can't see why any rational person would.

Here's some advice. If you want to learn about game design, you should play a game you hate with people who love it. And, rather than telling them how stupid the game is, try observing them. They really are having fun.

When I first heard the rules for *Killer Bunnies and the Quest for the Magic Carrot*, a popular hobby card game, I had no idea why it was fun. Here's the key mechanic: At the beginning of the game, you draw one "magic carrot" from a deck of 12. You set that card aside, in secret. Then you play with an entirely different deck of cards, trying to be the player who gets the matching carrot. Whoever gets it wins. That's right, the entire game comes down to one lottery draw, and your goal is to collect as many lottery tickets as you can.

In the endgame, the winning carrot is revealed by a process of elimination. Rather than just rolling a die at the end (which would give you the equivalent result, and might even feel somewhat less futile than selecting the key card at the beginning), you turn over every carrot that is not the magic carrot, and eliminate those lottery tickets from consideration. At the bottom of the pile, you find the winning carrot, and the player with the matching card wins.

You could achieve the same result in three seconds. But somehow, the triviality of the resolution does not diminish the appeal of the game. I watched players enjoying this game, and could not immediately explain why they were having fun. I felt like Jane Goodall. Over time, they came to trust me, and they invited me into their circle. And here is what I learned.

It does not matter who wins.

Killer Bunnies is a story, not a contest. The point is to play the game, not to win it. The cards are funny. The interactions are funny. People are funny. Even the suspenseful counting-off of the losing carrots is funny. If players had to work at this game, they would not have time to enjoy it.

Believe it or not, most people seek out games as entertainment, not as a challenge. They play to escape, not to engage. They want to hang out with their friends, not to dominate them. And thinking too hard will wreck that groove.

Yes, I know it's hard to swallow, but it really doesn't matter who wins. Obviously, if you ask a gambler "Do you want to win?" he will say yes. But if you watch him, you will see that it really doesn't make much difference. He plays until he runs out of money, or out of time. If losing actually mattered, he would do something else.

WHAT MAKES A GOOD GAMBLING GAME?

If gambling is more about entertainment than challenge, and if it doesn't matter who wins, how does a designer craft a new gambling game?

A good gambling game should be familiar, clear, easy, and volatile. Familiarity, the first of these, is the toughest nut to crack. As a designer you are always struggling to create something new. When you are breaking into the casino space, this urge will work against you. If you are inventing a new gambling game for your RPG, you can take a few more chances.

Familiarity

There are three paths to familiarity. The first is to be variation on a traditional game. The classic casino games have extremely long pedigrees: blackjack, craps, roulette, baccarat. Every now and then a traditional non-gambling game makes its way into the casino, as in the case of casino war. When new variations to these games come out, players already know most of the rules.

The second path to familiarity is to be famous. This is similar to being traditional, but it can happen in a shorter time. For most poker players, Texas hold 'em was a complete mystery until the mid-'90s. Then several things happened to catapult it into the spotlight. The "hole cam" made poker interesting to watch; casinos figured out how to make no-limit poker accessible to players with small bankrolls, through tournaments and limited buy-ins; and the Internet taught a whole new generation of card sharks how to play. By

2001, casino poker rooms had transformed from being mostly 7-card stud to mostly hold 'em.

The third way to familiarity is to build known mechanics in a new game. It's hard to do this without overdoing it, especially on the casino floor. Once in a while, you will see a more-or-less new game sneak into casinos and take hold, like a slot machine based on collapsing gems. Disappearing gems are familiar to any player who has played *Bejeweled* or other match-3 games. And even though the slot mechanics are quite different, the familiar parts of these games are sufficient to hook the player into learning the rest.

Clarity

Craps is a raucous game. Everyone cheers when the dice stop. Why is this? Because it is so immediately clear what each roll means. This "craps moment" is a good thing to put into in any game. Players can instantly process the information that the game is giving them. If this took a few seconds, the game would fall flat.

The moving parts of your game need to be simple, and their functionality must be so clear, that a player who sees the game for the first time believes he understands exactly how it works. He needs to believe this even if it's wrong.

Here's what I mean. *Wheel of Fortune* is one of the most successful slot machines in Las Vegas. Some people believe this is because of its association with a popular game show. But this alone is not the reason, because similarly-branded machines have done much worse.

The most alluring component of *Wheel of Fortune* is also the simplest: it's the big spinning wheel on the top of the machine. This wheel spins whenever you trigger the bonus game, which is easy to do: you just need to get a "spin" symbol on the third reel. (This is brilliant by itself, but I'll leave that up to you.)

When the big wheel spins, you get an award based on where it stops. These awards are printed on the wheel. There are no bad spots, no "bankrupt." There is just money, money, and more money. As much as a thousand credits. This mechanic is incredibly clear. But it is also a lie.

Like the reels themselves, the big wheel is biased. It does not hit each stop with equal frequency. It favors the smaller awards. There's real dissent among the casino gaming community about whether this specific deception is ethical. Clearly it is legal. But importantly, the perception of fairness on that wheel is what makes the game so attractive.

If you're designing a gambling game for a small play group, you probably don't need this layer of deception. If you're trying to put one in a casino, you probably do. Either way, the players must be clear on what they can do in the game, and how the game is supposed to respond.

Ease of play

Along with being familiar and clear, your game needs to be easy and fast to play. Some gambling games are over in less than a second. A hand of poker takes a minute and a half. Nearly all games in this category fall somewhere between those two extremes. Yes, a minute and a half is long.

Decisions in these games need to be extremely simple, if there are any decisions at all. This does not mean that they have to be easy (quite the contrary, in some cases), but the options must be clear. For example, optimal play at video poker requires the memorization of roughly a 100-hand chart, which differs for each variety of pay table. The choice is simple: hold zero to five of these cards. Making the correct choice is somewhat harder. But to play a hand of video poker, you do one simple thing: hold some of the cards.

Volatility

Something amazing ought to happen once in a while, or your game will be no fun. Every casino game has some degree of volatility. Even in blackjack, basically a 50/50 game, you can split, re-split, and double, not to mention hot and cold multi-hand streaks. Roulette numbers pay 35 to 1. Slot jackpots are all over the place. And even poker rooms award bonus jackpots based on high hands and bad beats, to add more excitement to that game.

Volatility is crucial because it increases a player's perception that he can beat the game. For an extremely bad case, consider a game with 99% payback and zero volatility. That is, for every dollar you put in, you withdraw 99 cents, guaranteed. This game has "great odds" but of course, it's terrible, because it's so clear how the story will go.

At the other end of the spectrum is a game like "100 or nothing," a real slot game with just one award: 100 credits. You spend a lot of your time earning nothing on this machine (more than 99 times out of 100). For most players, this award schedule is also pretty tiresome.

The trick, then, is to create a set of awards that cover the spectrum between frequent and large. Slots and video poker machines are exemplars of this approach. Video poker, for example, has an award at nearly every level that could get the player back to even in just one hand, each with a progressively lower chance of hitting.

THE HOUSE ADVANTAGE

While it's true that most gambling games have a built-in advantage for the house, it's beyond the scope of this article to teach you how to build it in. Balanced peer-to-peer games, such as poker, have no house advantage unless the casino takes a rake or a seat charge. Balanced games are easier to construct because they provide the same choices to every player. In a house-banked game, such as blackjack, the player and dealer play by different rules, and the odds are computed using an analysis of perfect play, which (considering the amount of information available to the player) is complicated indeed.

If you are designing a game for a casino, you will have to do this math at some point. If you're designing one for your own entertainment, you can be a little more casual.

SUMMARY

The experience of gambling is not really about who won; it is about what happened. Players like to be part of the story where they had a chance at a big win, even if most of the time they lose their money. And there's no better way to feel invested in something than to really have money on the line.

Over the last 40 years, slot machines have become the most popular gaming device on the casino floor. In part, this is because they are automated. But it's also because they are very good at telling stories. You bet a dollar, hit a bonus game, go through doors, find treasures, rescue a princess, and win 90 cents. You're like the players in *Killer Bunnies*: you just saw something wonderful happen. It's almost immaterial that it cost you a dime.

As a side note, yes, I know that there are gambling addicts. Anything that is easy, fun, and dangerous can become an addiction. If you design a fun gambling game, it will likely be fun for those players, too. And there is not much you can do about it. However, I think it's safe to say that the majority of your audience is casual gamblers, not gambling addicts. So focus on designing a good game for them.

Part 3
Development

In which we balance, test, rewrite, rebalance, retest, rewrite, and repeat until our games are the best they can be.

Developing Dominion

What Game Development Is All About
by Dale Yu

Not many games make every other designer insanely jealous. Rio Grande Games's Dominion is one of those games. It took the gaming world by surprise in 2008, outselling everything and winning every award. Dale Yu was on Dominion's development team, so I've asked him to share with us how it all came together. Mostly because I wanted to know. Fair warning: This essay contains rules specific to Dominion, and Dale doesn't waste space explaining them. If you don't know how to play it, take this opportunity to learn. Because honestly, if you're a designer, you can't not know how to play Dominion.

In the long process from initial prototype to published game, most game designs go through a development stage. Game development is one of the final steps that a board game must go through prior to publication. To paraphrase BASF: Game developers don't design a lot of the games you buy, they make a lot of the games you buy better....

In the development stage, the designer's final game submission is prepared to ready it for market by the developer. Rough edges are smoothed over, and the rules are tweaked to ensure a good game experience. Usually, the main ideas and mechanics of a game are unchanged through development—though just about anything is fair game to be modified if the change will result in a better game.

When my family members or other non-gamers ask what I do as a developer, I explain it this way: "Think of my job as being similar to that of a book editor, except that I work with board games instead of books. I take the prototype (manuscript) from the game designer (author), and then go over everything with a fine-toothed comb. My goal is to make sure that the published version is the best possible game for the company that will publish it." I'm always quick to point out that there is a huge difference between a game *developer* and a game *designer*. The inspiration for the game and the bulk of the original ideas come from the designer. The developer takes these ideas and creates a finished product from them.

Although there is no set "development pathway" that outlines what needs to be done for every game, there are a few things that commonly occur in the development process. I'll discuss those here, and I'll include a few examples that came up as I was developing *Dominion* along with my development partner, Valerie Putman.

INITIAL PLAYTESTING

The first thing that I do when I get a new project is to play the game using the rules provided. If possible, I learn the game straight from the rules and avoid getting any help or strategy tips from the designer or players who have played before. These initial plays will be my only opportunity to play the game as a "newbie," and I'd like to have that newbie experience as much as possible. For the first two or three plays, I simply play the game, trying to figure out the different workable strategies on my own. As I'm learning the game, I will write down any questions that arise while we learn the game. I also note the basic strategies used by the players and which ones were successful. Finally, I note any mechanics that feel awkward or that we needed to refer back to the rules to figure out.

Once I have a few game sessions under my belt, I'll take a step back and review individual mechanics. I'd like to see that every component of gameplay is a necessary part of the game, and I'd like to ensure that each mechanic works as simply as possible. Overly complicated elements in a game are often misunderstood or mislearned, and this leads to a bad game experience. So, wherever possible, I keep things simple. While we were working on *Dominion*, the game initially came with two "empty" cards—the Curse (cost 0, worth –1 victory point) and the Confusion (cost 0, worth 0 victory points). While it was nice to have two cards that could muck up your opponent's deck, it just seemed to be too much. There was no reason to have two different cards which had such similar effects. So the decision was made to only have the Curse, and this seems to have kept the game streamlined.

Once I've identified the areas of the game that I'd like to work on, I'll play a few more games focusing on these individual mechanics or strategies. I am continually evaluating the game mechanics to make sure that they work and that they are simple. I also make a mental list of the main possible strategies and play them all. With *Dominion*, we evaluated different card combinations to see if one was consistently winning. Then, to balance things out, one of us would specifically play that strategy while the rest of us would come up with ways to win using some other approach. Even the very strong deck-thinning strategy focused around the Chapel card proved to be nowhere near invincible—and therefore, Chapel stayed in the game.

This is also the stage of development where I push the boundaries to unmask any flaws in the game. Essentially, I come up with the most extreme strategies I can think of to try to break the game. I know that most of the ideas that I come up with will have no chance to win, but I need to know that the game can still function (and be fun) even if one player decides to buy all of one particular commodity, hoard as many cards as possible, or any other such strategy.

We made a big breakthrough in the development of *Dominion* when we tried a strategy that is now known as the Duchy Rush. In the initial stage of the game, *Dominion* ended when any one of the three Victory stacks were depleted. So, the Duchy Rush strategy had a simple algorithm: buying nothing if you had 0 to 2 coins in your hand, buying a Silver if you had 3 or 4 coins in your hand, and buying a Duchy if you had 5 or more coins in your hand. That's it. This strategy totally ignored all of the Kingdom cards on the table—and the Kingdom cards were supposed to be the big attraction of the game! Anyways, the Duchy Rush strategy turned out to be essentially unbeatable. The only way to beat it was to join in the strategy. So, to bring the Kingdom cards back in, the ending conditions were changed so that the game ended when either the Provinces were depleted or any three piles in the supply. We additionally increased the value of the Provinces from 5 victory points to 6. Now, there was definitely incentive to go for the higher valued Province cards. And the new end condition allowed the game to last long enough that players could develop a deck containing Kingdom cards and compete against someone who was buying up all the Duchies.

I will also set up highly improbable scenarios—creating a perfect storm of card draws, for example—to see how the rules handle these extreme conditions. Even if there is a situation that comes up once in a thousand games that "breaks" the game, you need to find that in development. Because if it makes it through to the final product, once someone discovers this broken situation, no matter how improbable, the online world will only focus on this flaw, and it will likely spell ruin for your game. One notable exception to this is *Balloon Cup*, a game in the 2-player line from Kosmos, which had a situation where the game could completely lock up. Despite this, a quick rules fix was published, and the game continued on to be nominated for Spiel des Jahres that year. But that is definitely the exception rather than the rule....

Pushing the boundaries of the game helps make sure that there are no "groupthink" strategies. As games are being designed, they are often played repeatedly by the designer and his or her game group. As they are all familiar with the game, their group may develop habits or tendencies in how they approach the game. The risk is that there may be strategies or situations that did not come up in the designer's playtesting, which can be exposed when someone is intentionally trying to break the game or when a complete newbie plays it without any preconceptions of the "right" way to play. In either event, the developers need to examine the game from all angles to make sure that the game doesn't break down when the unexpected happens.

RULES

Once the major game mechanics are set, then it's time to focus on the rules. For me, the rules are of paramount importance because when a gamer is first introduced to the game, the rules are the only way that I have to communicate with them. The rules must be easy to read and understand, and there have to be enough illustrations and examples for any gamer to be able to play the game. Including a reference card, if possible, is also a big plus for me. Of course, with *Dominion*, we didn't include a reference card—instead, we were able to come up with a pretty good mnemonic for the three phases of each turn: "A-B-C," for "Action, Buy, Cleanup." We highlighted this in the rules, and it turned out be a great way to help people remember what they are supposed to do each turn. Playtesting showed us that we didn't need a reference to remind people of the sequence as they were able to chant "A-B-C" during their turns.

Now, I'm not a graphic designer, so I leave the actual layout to someone else…but I definitely make sure that I keep an eye on how the layout process is going to ensure that the rules remain easy to read. Every time that I get a new version of the rules, I read every word making sure that no typos have slipped in.

BLIND PLAYTESTING

Once the main mechanics and rules are set, I usually embark on another round of playtesting to make sure that everything works. This next stage is the proving ground of development: the blind playtest. At this point, the game should be polished enough that any group should be able to pick it up and learn how to play it from the rules. And that's exactly what I try to do here.

I will give the game to a group of players, all of whom are new to the game, and ask them to read the rules, set up the game, and play. While I'll be present to watch them play, I tell them that I won't be able to answer any questions that may arise—if they have issues, they'll have to refer to the rulebook as the only authority. Of course, I'm there taking notes during the whole game recording where playtesters had issues with the setup and gameplay, and whether or not the rules were sufficient to answer those questions. Essentially, I'm trying to simulate a "first game" for a game group. First impressions are still the most important impressions to make, so I want to see that a group of gamers can get up and running with the game on their own.

At the end of the game, I'll have a bunch of questions to ask the playtesters. First, I need to know if they enjoyed the game, and if they thought it was fun. Second, I'll ask them about any issues they had with the rules or mechanics. Finally, I'll ask them if they think that anything can be improved. While most of the mechanics should be set at this point, you never know if an outsider might have some brilliant simplification of a rule or mechanic. In the same way that I'm worried about the designer's group having groupthink, I'd also like to try to make sure that my own group did not fall into the same groupthink trap!

After each game, it's time to put some more work back into the game— fixing up the rules if needed or tweaking things in the game itself based on the comments of the playtesters. In our work on *Dominion*, we were most focused on making sure that people could learn the game from the rules. There were a number of small but important timing rules (such as when to shuffle your discard pile), which were critical in making sure the game worked as intended.

We spent a lot of time working on the wording and illustrations in the rules to make sure that the gamers could understand these finer points of the rules.

We also worked very hard in this phase of *Dominion*'s development choosing cards to recommend for the First Game. In the same way that we wanted the rules to be easy enough to understand, we wanted to choose a set of cards that would get novice players up and running as soon as possible. The first thing we knew for sure is that the First Game couldn't include Curses. They simply slowed the game down too much, and they would be too much to handle for a new player. We also found that many of our blind playtesters got stuck with hands filled with terminal actions. Players were very frustrated to draw a hand of five Action cards, but not have any additional actions so that they could only choose one of the five cards to play, and then they had to discard the rest. From this experience, we learned that we needed to include as many cards with +1 Action as we possibly could so that novices would likely have a number of options with each hand regardless of which cards they bought. After we had set those two important parameters, we then chose cards to get every important term (Action, Buy, Trash, Draw, Reaction, Attack, Gain, etc.) in that first set of cards, so that players would be familiar with as much of the game as possible after that first game.

TITLE AND THEMING

The final facet of the development stage was coming up with an appropriate theme and title. Although some games are completely built around a theme (that is, the story comes first and then a game is built around the constraints of that story), most games can be viewed in an abstract sense and then any theme can be "pasted" on to it. Again taking the example of *Dominion*, it is essentially a deck-building game. The theme and feel of the game comes from the titles of the card and the art. If Rio Grande Games had wanted a game with an outer space theme, Roman theme, or Egyptian theme, the card titles and art could have easily been molded to fit any of those concepts. At that time, Rio Grande Games had recently published *Race for the Galaxy*, which was set in outer space, so that pretty much eliminated that option. There had also been a recent glut of Roman- and pirate-themed games at that time, so we shied away from those themes as they seemed a bit stale at that point. As it turns out, the cards came to us with a medieval-ish theme, and this seemed like a good fit, so we didn't change it at all.

Once we had settled on the medieval theme, the last piece of the puzzle was coming up with a suitable title. The designer of the game gives most of his prototypes basic descriptive names. The initial name of the game was "Castle Builder." Although this name certainly helped people quickly identify it from all his other prototypes, it wasn't particularly catchy. It was difficult coming up with a title that evoked the sense of building that was central to the game, kept to the medieval theme, and wasn't already in use by another game.

I quickly thought of the title *Dominion*, which the dictionary defines as:

1. *Control or the exercise of control; sovereignty; or*

2. *A territory or sphere of influence or control; a realm.*

This met the criteria I had set out looking for a title, and it had the added benefit of not being tied to a particular time period. This became important with later expansions as the name did not limit us to any specific time frame or theme.

CONCLUSION

Development is an important but often underappreciated part of a game's overall production. What needs to happen in this stage is extremely variable—dependent on the original prototype, dependent on the needs of the publisher, and dependent on the current gaming market. The developer is charged with taking the prototype, looking at it from a different perspective than the designer, and readying it for production. Some games may need a complete overhaul while others may not need much work at all. However, the development process is important in either case to make sure that the game is polished and meets the needs of the publisher. When the game feels "fully developed," that's when you know you've added something of value.

Dale Yu *is the co-developer of the deckbuilding game Dominion, and its expansions Intrigue, Alchemy, Seaside, Prosperity, and Cornucopia. He is a columnist for boardgamenews.com, an administrator on boardgamegeek.com, and the founder and editor of opinionatedgamers. com. When he's not writing about board games, Dale is a physician in Cincinnati.*

Thinking Exponentially

The Tricky Task of Imbalancing Collectible Games

by Paul Peterson

*When I need someone to make a game, I might turn to any of the fine designers in this book. But when I need someone to **break** a game, I turn to Paul Peterson. Paul got into his first R&D job the old-fashioned way: by just being as good at that department's games as any of the people in it. As* Magic: The Gathering's *original "Mr. Suitcase," he showed he can hold a universe of collectible objects in his head, contrasting strengths and weaknesses, like few others in the game industry. Here, he tells us how he controls the vast store of information needed to make a sprawling collectible game.*

One goal of creating any game is to make sure that it is "balanced." Players should feel as though they had an equal chance to win the game given the same rules and resources as other players. This can be tricky enough in a game where all of the components come in a single package. For collectible games it is even harder. A number of challenges must be overcome.

The primary challenge is one of numbers. Most other challenges are related to this subject either directly, or indirectly. Large numbers of components help drive the collectible aspect of the game, and also ensure that there are many different ways to play the game which makes it more fun. However, large numbers of components also create an exponentially large number of possible interactions, and each of those interactions, even between two properly balanced components, has the potential to be unbalanced.

Large numbers of components also require a game to be more complex. Each game component needs to be unique in some way for it to be collectible. Once all of the basic mechanics have been created, each new one must get more complex. Balancing complex components against other complex components creates even more difficult interactions and compounds the problem.

The solution to this challenge is to fight numbers with numbers. It is primarily about putting in the time to test as many of the combinations of possible, but it is also a matter of doing so intelligently. Identify the most dangerous components in the game; the ones with the most complex abilities or that involve large changes in the game. Then concentrate on testing those thoroughly. Then move on to the next most dangerous ones and repeat. Over time, experience will make the process easier.

Having more testers also helps not only because you can test more interactions in the same amount of time but also because different people will find different problems. It is vital to remember that ten thousand fans will play a game more in a single day than ten designers will in six months. They will find ways to play that the game's designers never dreamed of.

Organizing all of this data is a challenge in itself, but it is vital. Recording matchups and win/loss records for tests can help identify problems more quickly and track whether the solutions are working. Databases allow comparisons between current component design and previous ones to help prevent duplication or unwanted power increases. Designers need to embrace all the tools available to make their games as fun as possible.

The second challenge for balancing these games is with the idea of "costing," and how to deal with the necessary granularity of it. Using components in games always has a cost, even if players don't think about it. In a game like *Magic: The Gathering* some costs are obvious, such as the amount of mana a player must spend to play a card. That cost is very granular. Each card must be assigned an amount of mana based on the set of mechanics it has. It also has unobvious costs, such as the value of a card in a player's hand, deck size, and many others. All contribute to value, but the cost is the most important.

This can make balancing many of the cards very difficult. A card's "value" can easily fall somewhere between the costing options available. At one cost it's better than other similar cards and at the next highest cost it's worse. Some cards can be tweaked by changing their abilities slightly to make them fit better, but with others it is a matter of deciding whether to release a slightly worse card or a slightly better one.

The costing challenge has an easy solution, though; release the cards anyway. Some of them will be slightly good and some of them will be slightly bad. Or some of them will be quite good and others will be quite bad.

Imperfect balance isn't necessarily bad. In the HeartGold and SoulSilver set for the *Pokémon Trading Card Game*, there is a card called Bill that allows the player to "Draw two cards." In the Undaunted expansion for that same set the card Team Rocket Trickery allows the player to "Draw two cards. Then, your opponent discards a card from his or her hand." For many designers, this is heresy. They'll say you should never have one card that is strictly better than another. However, when examined in more realistic terms, there are many reasons why such a card may be made.

The strongest reason to create two cards such as these is to help players get more of a particular effect that they like in a single deck. Most collectible games have rules about how a player puts their game pieces together. In *Pokémon* (and many other trading card games), players are limited to four of a single card in their deck. Two different cards with similar effects allow the player to get around those rules. This is truer in more hardcore games such as *Magic*, where deck construction is more closely followed, and players will gladly put Shock in their deck alongside Lightning Bolt, even though Shock does one less damage for the same cost.

Another reason to create these cards is to support the individual releases. If you expect players to play with limited set of cards and want to make sure they have a specific ability in each set, then you either have to reprint the card with that ability or make a new, similar card. It could even be the case that in a particular set that ability is weaker or stronger and needs to be adjusted to fit properly, which can lead to exactly this situation.

There are other options than making strictly better or worse cards, though. If Bill also had a second ability that was different than Team Rocket Trickery's, then the comparison would be much more difficult. The number of red *Magic* cards that were printed that cost two mana, deal three damage, and have an additional ability is truly staggering, and made direct comparisons difficult. However, there is a lot of value in a simple ability like "Draw two cards," and adding lots of extra abilities on top of it just to be different increases the complexity of the game.

There are other ways in which imbalanced components can help a game. They generate excitement, for one. Cards like Black Lotus and Time Walk helped showcase the possibilities for *Magic* when it came out. *Yu-Gi-Oh!* and *Pokémon* thrive on the excitement generated by their powerful rare cards, which are often strictly better than other cards. Players love to seek out the imbalances in a game. It makes them feel smart and powerful.

The real trick is controlling the imbalance, not destroying it. A defining characteristic of collectible games is that they continuously release content. This gives a designer the ability to change the environment of the game over time. Strategically using imbalance is a powerful tool for this change.

One problem in complex games is that a single strategy can quickly dominate the way the game is played. By creating components that are better than average in a competing strategy and releasing them in the next set, a designer can bolster it and make it competitive. Players will quickly identify the new strategy and begin playing it, and the game will be better for the competition. Designers can also create cards that specifically foil an undesirable (or, in *Magic*-speak, "degenerate") strategy, and release them into the environment. Since their use is more limited, they can be fairly strong and still not be severely unbalanced. Care must be taken with this tactic, as bolstering one tactic to stop another can create an arms race where the new tactic needs a foil, which needs a foil, and so on till Doomsday.

There are some tricks to making "properly imbalanced" components as well. The first one is learning to create "combos." Combos are when the interactions of two pieces are strong because of the way their mechanics work together. Either piece on its own can be perfectly balanced, but when they are used together their whole is greater than the sum of their parts. Once a designer learns to find the ones they create by accident, they can also start to see how to make them on purpose.

In general, a properly constructed combo can be very powerful without spoiling the fun of a game. This is because it requires effort and luck to make the combo work in the first place. In *Magic*, for example, a player has to get the exact cards they need and be able to use them both in order to make the combo work. In a 60-card deck this can be tricky, and so they must bring in even more cards to help them get the combo they are looking for. The more cards the combo requires to create, the stronger it can be. When it does happen it will make the player feel great for having done it, but it will be unlikely to dominate play over all because of how difficult it is to make happen.

One trick that does not work is making rare components more powerful. Many designers feel that the fact that these items are harder to get means that they can be more powerful. The only time this would ever be true is if a product is failing. Otherwise it should be assumed that anyone who wants to play at the highest level has every card they need. Making the rares more powerful just devalues all of the other cards and makes the game about who can spend the most money. It is also true, however, that many of the "properly imbalanced" card may end up as rares because they represent complex mechanics and limited use cases that do not belong with the common cards. There is a big difference between this and purposely creating tiers of power based on rarity.

Collectible games are some of the most complex games to create and balance. The number of possible interactions that are created when the players can choose which components to use in a game is immense, and tracking those interactions and balancing the game around them is a daunting task. The good news is that such games are quite robust and the ability to constantly release new content for them gives a lot of power to the designer to change the game environment as it evolves.

Paul Peterson *has been a designer and developer on many collectible games such as Magic: The Gathering, Pokémon, BattleTech, Vampire: The Eternal Struggle, Clout Fantasy, and Bella Sara, as well as traditional card games like Guillotine and Unexploded Cow. He has also worked on massively multiplayer roleplaying games, PC games, and games for social networks.*

Stealing the Fun

by Dave Howell

Over the years, I've been lucky to hear Dave Howell's "Golden Guidelines for Game Design" come together as Dave has thought of them. Many members of our circle of designers have internalized Dave's guidelines as gospel, and can hear his voice in our head when we go astray. I can't put them all in here, because that's an entire book. Which I hope Dave finishes someday. But for now, he's here to talk about whether the fun you think is in your game is still all there when you're done playing.

Have you ever been stuck in one of those games where you've added up your points or calculated your unit strength or looked at your hand, and realized that, although the game isn't over yet, there's no possible way for you to win? So you have to spend the rest of the game being a "good sportsman," playing as if you care about the outcome, when you really just want to tell the guy across the table who's carefully looking at every card in his hand, "C'mon! Just pick one and play it! It doesn't matter anyway! Geez!"

I know I have. I've also played games where I wasn't necessarily guaranteed to lose, but it sure seemed that way, and finishing the game felt more like a chore than anything else. There are a number of ways that a game can steal the fun and leave a player with a bad taste in their mouth, but they all come out of one really important principle:

A game is not fun unless a player believes they have some reasonable chance to win until the moment the game ends.

Yeah, yeah, there are some freakishly rare exceptions. Some people will play a game they're practically guaranteed to lose because they'll learn something. Or they'll play to lose so that somebody else can be happy because they won (that is, "throw the game"). But in the normal world, 99.99% of all game players are playing to win, and because they think they can win.

Make sure you read the principle very carefully. For one thing, a player doesn't need a good chance to win. It can be a long shot. "Sure, I'm nearly a parsec behind the other players, but one of them might melt their engine, and another might hit a habitat or fall into a black hole; it could happen!" They just need some clutchable shred of hope in order to keep the fun alive.

Also, a player does not need to actually have "some reasonable chance" to win. They just have to believe that they do. It might really be 100,000 to 1 odds, or maybe if they remembered what the other players have in their "reserve stacks," they'd know it was hopeless. But as long as they think they have a chance to win, the game can be fun. So let's look at some of the ways that games screw this up. What does a game need to avoid doing in order to help preserve a player's belief that they have a reasonable chance to win, right up until the game ends?

GUIDELINE #1: DON'T KICK A PLAYER OUT BEFORE THE GAME IS OVER

The one surefire way to show a player that they don't have any chance of winning is to kick them out while the game's still going on. *Monopoly* is the poster child for this one. *Monopoly* also illustrates a corollary to Guideline #1, which is "Don't make a player wish they'd been kicked out." Long before Marco actually goes bankrupt and can leave the table, his financial situation is clearly poor enough that he knows he's going to lose. He has no reasonable chance of winning, but he's supposed to be a Good Sport and keep playing as if he might win, even though he'd much rather just strike a really cushy deal with some other player, sell out, and get out of the game.

Which leads us to Guideline #2...

GUIDELINE #2: KINGMAKING SUCKS

"Kingmaking" is when a player is in a position to choose who gets to win the game, but cannot pick themselves. It comes in three different flavors.

Guideline #2a: Never create a kingchooser

In the hypothetical game *Nine Rings of Maughbel*, Bonnie must draw a card and then pass it either to Amarion on her left or Christine on her right. Bonnie draws...a ring. Amarion and Christine both have eight rings, so Bonnie's next move will make one of them win the game.

For whatever reason, Bonnie gives the card to Amarion. Does he get to enjoy the win, knowing that all the previous effort he'd put into the game had come down to merely a mental coin flip, or because Bonnie is his girlfriend? Probably not. Since Bonnie had no strategic or tactical reason, no in-game reason whatsoever, to pick one or the other, Christine feels that they might as well have just dealt out playing cards to see who got the ace of spades first. It'd have been a lot faster than playing this dumb game.

Guideline #2b: Don't reward a kingmaker

If a game robs a player of the hope of winning, then it really ought to avoid making it more fun to lose by throwing the game. *Risk* is the classic example of this. Damian is one of three players left in the game, and he's clearly the weakest. What he's supposed to do is keep fortifying his position, shrinking down as the other players attack him to win their bonus cards, until one of them thinks they can wipe him off the board, take his remaining cards, and thus win the game. I've never actually seen that happen. Instead, Damian, who's tired of waiting to be killed, will make a kamikaze attack on Ed. Damian won't be able to eliminate Ed, and the attack will leave both of them so weak that Fiona will crush them, but it was a heck of a lot more fun than just sitting there.

Guideline #2c: Try to avoid a kingbreaker

The mildest of the kingmaking sins, a kingbreaker is somebody who can steal the win from another player. Gregor and Hiroto are neck and neck at the finish line, with Jamal right behind. Li is half a lap back. Li plays a Tack In Road card on Gregor, even though there's no reasonable chance that it will let Li win the game. It's now going to be either Hiroto or Jamal.

Now, if that card were Tacks All Over Road and everybody had to roll to see who avoided them, that's a different matter. The dice, not Li, are deciding who blows a tire, and hey, maybe everybody would, and Li might, just might, be able to catch up. Much better!

Kingbreaking is perilously close to some good game design elements, so it's very hard to entirely avoid. Generally, good sportsmanship on the part of the players can keep it from spoiling a game.

So, a kingchooser is forced to pick somebody to win the game. A kingmaker can hand the win to another player. A kingbreaker can take the win from another player. It's commonly accepted that "kingmaking is bad," but it's important to understand the variations, and why some are much worse than others.

GUIDELINE #3: DON'T REWARD THE LEADER

The first car into the pit should not be able to take the "best" position; the highest scoring player for the last hand shouldn't get to choose their cards first for the next. That's "snowballing," and it's bad. If taking an early lead lets a player control more resources, the other players will be ready to quit as soon as somebody pulls into the lead. Chalk up another failure for *Monopoly* on this one; "the rich get richer" might be realistic, but it's not much fun.

Many really good games take this idea a step further, and actually punish the leader. This should be modest, and preferably subtle, but most of my favorite games have a "headwind" mechanism. Take *MarioKart*, for example. Of the "special" power-ups that can be collected, some (the banana peel) are more effective when you're in the lead, and others (the red "homing" turtle shell grenade) work better when you're behind. The banana peel is quite weak, but the red shell is very strong; in general, the farther behind a player is, the more effective the bonus weapons are. A well-designed headwind really helps a player in the back believe that there's still a chance to win.

Another way to describe Guideline #3 is "snowballing bad, headwind good."

GUIDELINE #4: INCLUDE INHERENT DECELERATION

The closer a player is to the end of the game, the greater the uphill climb should be. It's easy to confuse this one with Guideline #3. The difference is that a headwind affects the player(s) in the lead, no matter how close to the finish line they are, but inherent deceleration affects everybody, but affects people near the finish line more.

Settlers of Catan has some beautifully subtle deceleration. Players are trying to get 10 victory points. The first two are so easy to get, that you have them already on your very first turn. The next couple aren't very hard either. If you're strong in brick and wood, you get them with more roads and settlements. If you're strong in stone and grain, you upgrade to a city, or go for Biggest Army. But whichever way you go, you can't get all the way to 10 points in one direction. There are only five settlements to play, so at some point you'll have to upgrade some of them to cities; on the other hand, you can't upgrade to cities and win without also building more settlements to upgrade. The last couple of victory points have to be earned by doing whatever wasn't easy enough to do for the first 5 or 6. Ergo, a player with 4 victory points is much closer to one with 6 than a player with 7 victory points is to one with 9.

Phase 10 is a rummy-like card game. Players are trying to create a specific group of cards during a hand, called a set. If a player completes a set, then on the next hand, they move down the list to create the next set. Players who fail must try to create the same set on the next hand. The early sets are easy, so if one player is on Set #2, they aren't very far behind a player trying to complete Set #4. The later sets are much harder, so moving through Sets #8, #9, and #10 are very difficult, and a player that's two sets back in the late stages is farther behind than they might think. As a bonus, *Phase 10*'s steps also provide a headwind. Since a hand ends shortly after any player completes a set, if there are players still trying to complete lower sets, they will tend to cause hands to finish more quickly, before players on higher sets can finish their tasks, which gives the lower players more of a chance to catch up.

Inherent deceleration primarily creates the illusion of a reasonable chance of winning: near the end of a game, players will think they're closer to the leader than they really are. This is exactly what you want in order to encourage them to believe they still have a reasonable chance of winning.

GUIDELINE #5: A PLAYER'S ABILITY TO INFLUENCE OTHER PLAYERS SHOULD FALL BETWEEN "NONE" AND "LOTS"

No player interaction means you're playing group solitaire, but too much means a player in the lead is just the first to get crushed. A lot of players and designers have trouble putting their finger on this one, especially since some games may not reveal a problem with too much influence until you've played them enough to figure out all the different ways you can mess with other players, and beware the "nice" playtest group that doesn't take full advantage of opportunities to gang up on the leader.

Different players like different amounts of influence. *Lunch Money* has "lots and lots"; too much for my taste, but some people really like it. *Rack-O*, on the other hand, has none. Each player is playing a solitaire game, with the only interaction being the win condition: whoever completes their game in the fewest moves wins. This is similar to *Race for the Galaxy* (unless you're using the takeover rules), except that *RftG* does have some carefully engineered indirect influence: which game phase you choose to play, and which cards you throw out. I've seen quite a few published games that had little or no interaction, but I haven't ever seen a great game that did.

This is also closely related to Guideline #3, because when players can affect each other, they'll usually try to drag back whoever's in the lead, for obvious reasons. If the game mechanics don't provide an inherent headwind, often the players will.

GUIDELINE #6: DON'T FORCE A REVERSE

It's perfectly all right to give somebody a choice of reducing their score to buy something, but to force somebody to go backwards on the track, or to lose money, or have points subtracted, is more frustrating than making everybody else's points go up, even if the result is functionally identical. Imagine a game about racing to the South Pole. An event like "Blizzard: players without extra tent stakes slide backwards six spaces" is more frustrating than "Blizzard: players without snow goggles lose their next two turns." It's just how people think.

That's the simple version of that guideline. In practice, applying it has caveats, because sometimes a game *needs* a way to move one player backwards. If you find yourself in this situation (well, it's more a matter of "when" than "if"), there are a number of ways to reduce the pain.

Think about sporting events. Hockey, football, basketball, rugby, downhill skiing, whatever. How often do you see the scoreboard count backwards? Almost never. But nearly all sports have mechanisms for penalizing the players. Football sometimes forces a reverse by moving the team further from their goal, but deducting from their position isn't as direct as deducting from their score. In a horse racing game, lowering somebody's speed would be better than moving them backwards along the track.

Speaking of tracks, there's a whole class of games that is entirely about moving along a track: *Candy Land*, *Parcheesi*, *Sorry!*, and *Aggravation*, to name a few. There is no other resource besides track position. Particularly when each player has multiple pawns on the track, moving everybody else forward is just too complicated. I think the fact that one of the games is named *Aggravation* pretty much spells out why this class of games tends to be ignored by more sophisticated players.

Another excellent way to include reversals without all the pain is through money, for two reasons. First of all, players already have expectations about money; sometimes you have to pay a fine, or a toll, or an emergency repair.

Money comes pre-loaded with expectations of having to spend it, sometimes involuntarily. Another benefit comes from the usual way money is handled. In most games, you have a pile of money (bills or doubloons or credits), and it's not really easy to see how much money each player has relative to the others. If you're not sure who's got how much, being forced backwards (having to lose some money) isn't as painful. Finally, if players are dealing with a fairly wide range of denominations, losing a few bills or coins from a large pile doesn't seem like a major setback, even if it's a few big bills. Deep down, there's still part of the brain that would rather have seven nickels instead of two quarters, because seven is more monies than two.

So try not to force reverses, but if you need to, hide the reverse by applying it to a secondary resource, by applying it to a resource that's hard to compare against other players', by using a resource that's measured with a wide range of denominations, and/or by using a resource that players expect will be decremented on occasion.

Now, just because some particular game manages to steer around every single design flaw listed above doesn't mean anybody's going to enjoy playing it. You do need a game that is fun to start with, after all. It's just a shame when a game hands out big mugs full of fun, and then steals the fun back from a player after they've spent a couple hours playing the game. It's even more of a shame if a player feels that their fun has been stolen at the beginning of a game, but games like that tend to get thrown out pretty quickly. Still, don't make the mistake of thinking these guidelines are mostly applicable to the end of a game. Lots of major arbitrary events, game "cul-de-sacs" where players can get trapped, or even poorly written rules can put a player in a position of feeling like they no longer have any clear choices that might lead to victory.

There is a corollary to this principle, by the way, which is "A game is not fun unless a player believes they have some reasonable chance to lose until the moment the game ends." Playing a game where you take it for granted you are going to win is barely any better than playing one where you know you're going to lose (unless you're playing for money). Either way, the uncertainty of who will take the crown once the scores are added up is the heart of the principle. Keep that mystery alive for the players. Don't steal the fun.

Dave Howell *was a co-author of Wizards of the Coast's first published product, and later was a playtester, editor, and production manager for Magic: The Gathering. He's also credited as a playtester for at least 75% of all Cheapass Games, which is only somewhat related to the fact that he's the guy who gave James Ernest his first job in the game industry. This essay is excerpted from "Golden Guidelines of Game Design," a game design lecture he has presented at various conventions, featuring more than twenty guidelines for making better games.*

~~Writing Rules with Precision~~
~~Writing Rules Precisely~~
Writing Precise Rules

by Mike Selinker

I've redesigned, expanded, adapted, and creative-directed a lot of very big games: Axis & Allies, Dungeons & Dragons, Attack!, Risk, *and the like. Their rule sets are often similarly gigantic, which means they need special attention paid to clarity and purpose. Otherwise, I might get a game whose FAQ is longer than other games' entire rulebooks. Here, I'll go into what makes a rule set good, and what makes one not so good.*

I play games for a living. Writing rules is what I do for fun. Of all the things I like about being a game designer, the ability to craft something elegant is the one I enjoy most, because it's a difficult thing to do well.

I have a few rules writing maxims that I've never put in one place. They're about what you write when your game has made it out of the development phase and now needs to be played by people who aren't you. If you'd like to try them out, have a go.

I'll also introduce each of the ten maxims with a game rule that deserved some extra attention, but didn't get it.

USE NO INTERMEDIARY TERMINOLOGY

A hexagonal grid has been printed on the board to determine movement. Hereafter, these hexagons will be called "squares."

—Afrika Korps

I just made my geometry teacher roll over in his irregular hexahedron. Hexagons can be called many things—hexes, spaces, zones—but they cannot, under any circumstances, be called squares.

Call the thing what it is, and people will remember it just by looking at it. Those things in your dice bag are named by their number of faces: this is a 12-sider (or d12), that is a 20-sider (or d20). The first designers to use polyhedrals didn't call one the "breaker" and one the "thunderstriker." Placing intermediary names for things in the way of comprehension only obscures comprehension.

My design partner James Ernest and I were required by our publisher to convert a board game written in English to an internationally usable form. So the cards for *Gloria Mundi* were renamed into Latin, a language that everyone fails to speak equally. I went through and picked Latin names you could associate with English terms; for example, the Fish Market became the Piscatorium. But a much harder task was taking phrases such as "At the end of your turn, you may discard one Building card on the table (including the Marketplace) and replace it with the Shock Troops" and turning them into *symbols*. Eventually we cut all the complex cards to avoid requiring too much symbolic translation. The game got worse because of it, and now we're playing the game in English again.[26]

Properly used, symbols can be fine, but one symbol cannot do the work of ten. The excellent game *Bang!* took a cheater's way out that I would not advise. It put on many cards a little book symbol that just meant "See the rulebook." Yuck.

USE REAL WORDS

2.2401 GUN DUELS: Vs a non-concealed, non-Aerial DEFENDER's declared Defensive First Fire attack on it, a vehicle may attempt to Bounding First Fire (D3.3) its MA (/other-FP, including Passenger FP/SW) at that DEFENDER first, provided the vehicle need not change CA, is not conducting OVR (D7.1), its total Gun Duel DRM (i.e., its total Firer-Based [5.] and Acquisition [6.5] TH DRM for its potential shot) is < that of the DEFENDER, and the DEFENDER's attack is not Reaction Fire (D7.2). Neither the +1 DRM for a Gyrostabilizer nor the doubling of the lower dr for other ordnance in TH Case C4 (5.35) is included in the Gun Duel DRM calculation. The order of fire for non-ordnance/SW is determined as if it were ordnance [EXC: TH Case A can apply only if this unit/weapon is mounted-on/aboard a vehicle that is changing CA; all such non-turret-mounted fire is considered NT for purposes of TH Case C, and; A.5 applies to any type of FG]. If the ATTACKER's and DEFENDER's total Gun Duel DRM are equal, the lower Final TH (or non-ordnance IFT) DR fires first—and voids the opponent's return shot by eliminating, breaking, stunning, or shocking it. If those two Final DR are equal, both shots are resolved simultaneously. Any CA change the DEFENDER requires in order to shoot (5.11) is made before the ATTACKER's shot if the DEFENDER's total Gun Duel DRM.

—Advanced Squad Leader

If you're selling a game to English-speaking customers, there's no excuse for writing it in anything but English. *Advanced Squad Leader* is one of the greatest games of all time, but only if you have a Rosetta stone for the damn thing. Since it's my favorite wargame, I understand how to play it, and I also understand I would *never* let a new player try to learn from the rules.

---

[26] See also the great game *Race for the Galaxy*, where my friend Wei-Hwa Huang laid out the cards in bizarre symbols I'm sure he completely understood. This does not mean that I do. That said, I have not asked him whether he understands *Gloria Mundi's* symbols.

The rule above isn't a bad rule. It's actually a pretty good rule. It says, translated, that when a vehicle is attacked, it gets to return fire beforehand, but under some more limited circumstances and without all the bells and whistles. But the rule writers forgot that most people don't read rule books in order, and so they might not know what "attempt to Bounding First Fire (D3.3) its MA (/other-FP, including Passenger FP/SW)" means. They also believed that a phrase such as "Bounding First Fire" makes a good *verb*.

Once you have a real word for something, don't use any other word for it. Über-designer Jonathan Tweet has a maxim of his own: "Things are the same, or they are different." If you have called your attack a "salvo," it must always be a "salvo," and never an "attack." If that bothers you, maybe you should have just called it an "attack."

MAKE NO MORE WORK THAN NECESSARY

Fate [the gamemaster] then makes a percentile die roll to determine whether the empty ship will be safe or not. The first roll is a 33. This indicates there is only a 33% chance of the boat remaining safe. Fate then rolls again. The resulting roll of 40 indicates that their ship won't be there upon return. How and when the ship is lost is up to Fate.

—The World of Synnibarr

Yes, I know this is a board and card game design book, and I just quoted an RPG—and not just any RPG, but what some people believe is the worst RPG product ever. (It isn't. But it's close.) The *Synnibarr* rule commits a cardinal sin that bears noting for card games and board games, too: It requires the person administering the game to do more work than she needs to.

Let's say you're "Fate." (Cringe.) You need to know whether the ship is safe. The rules tell you to roll dice to establish the percentage chance of the ship being safe. Then the rules tell you to roll again, and if you roll equal to or under that percentage, the ship is lost. What is the chance the ship is safe? Your first roll will be between 1 and 100. Your second roll will be *the same thing*. So adding up the 1% chance you'll roll equal to or under a 1, and the 2% chance you'll roll equal to or under a 2, and so on up to the 100% you'll roll equal to or under a 100, then divide by 100…and you get 50.5%. In other words, it's a coin flip. So just tell the GM—I'm sorry, Fate—that there's a 50% chance the ship is gone, and she'll have to roll only once.

It's not just bad games that have this problem. When I helped reboot *Axis & Allies*, I looked at every rule to see how much effort the player was required to expend. In the 1986 version, there were two combat sequences: land combat and naval combat. That was just too burdensome. After weeks of rewriting and testing, we got it down to one sequence that included everything from anti-aircraft guns blasting Stukas out of the London sky, to submarines sinking merchant fleets off the coast of Japan. ("Figure 3-3. *Axis & Allies Terms*" on

Terms from Axis & Allies (1986)	Terms from Axis & Allies (2004)
an action	a phase
a battle	a combat
land (or naval) combat sequence	combat sequence
combat sphere action	combat action
naval combat	sea combat
attack capability or attack factor	attack
defense capability or defense factor	defense
counterattack	defend
enemy-controlled or enemy-occupied	hostile
allied	friendly
naval unit	sea unit
an infantry unit	an infantry
an artillery unit	an artillery
an armor unit	a tank
armor	tanks
plane	air unit
fighter plane	fighter
round of combat	cycle
first shot attack	sneak attack
support attack	bombardment
make a support attack	bombard
National Control Marker (NCM)	control marker
casualty line	casualty zone
I.P.C.	IPC
penalty	IPC loss
toss (a die)	roll
withdraw (a submarine)	submerge
island group	island
country or world power	power
capital territory	capital
take over	capture
item	unit
place on the board	mobilize
multi-player force	multinational force
kill	destroy

Figure 3-3. *Axis & Allies Terms*

page 93 shows more changes from one edition to the next; see if you can figure out why the changes were made.)

Look, administering rules is *work*. When a player is learning a game, she wants the simplest possible set of actions to figure out how to play. Cut out all the rules that require her to learn more.

ADD FLAVOR (BUT NOT TOO MUCH FLAVOR)

NATO has rules covering the use of tactical nuclear weapons. To simulate the use of strategic nuclear weapons simply soak the map with lighter fluid and apply a flame.

—*NATO: Operational Combat in Europe in the 1970's*

Jim Dunnigan felt comfortable writing that rule in 1973. I might not be able to get away with it now. That's something that looks like rules text, meaning a player might actually do it. (I know: only if they're dumb. Some players are dumb.)

Flavor text is usually kept outside the rules, often by italicizing it or boxing it or putting it into word balloons issuing from the mouths of cartoon characters. It's generally short and pithy, and often funny. In trading card games, it's usually found in italics below the card rules. For example, in the cyberpunk TCG *Netrunner*, there was a program card called Sphinx 2.0. I wrote, "What runs on four megs in the morning, two megs in the afternoon, and three megs in the evening?" When I stopped typing that, I knew that all work on that card's flavor text had ceased. I didn't need any more flavor than that, and the rest of the card could be ceded to the all-important rules.

Things get tricky when your flavor commingles with your rules. I once had an editor tell me that flavor and rules were like oil and water; they shouldn't be mixed. That editor was wrong. They're more like a Reese's Peanut Butter Cup; you can put them together, but you'd better know what you're doing first. For example, the game *Hatfields & McCoys*—a true-to-life simulation of Ozark bumpkin infighting—is written entirely in the following style:

If'n one o' the other player's Ellies is in the river, all yer Beaus within four spaces gotta mosey on over to her space and stack with her. Any Beaus who gets to her hasta fight while the rest o' the Beaus closeby just stands there a gawkin'.

That's completely comprehensible, once you get yourself a hankerin'...I mean, once you get into the right mindset. But you have to be there. It wouldn't be a good style for simulating the Battle of Thermopylae.

MAKE YOUR TEXT NO SMARTER THAN YOUR READER

The battlefield is usually produced by placing separate terrain features on a flat board or cloth representing flat good going such as pasture, open arable fields, steppe grassland or smooth desert. Alternatively, the player can provide permanent terrain boards or blocks incorporating equivalent features. The battlefield is now notionally bisected twice at right angles to its edge to produce 4 equal quarters.

—De Bellis Antiquitatis

"Notionally bisected twice at right angles to its edge to produce 4 equal quarters"? Did *DBA's* authors believe that if they'd said "cut into fourths," people would cut it into four triangles? The added specificity makes the game read like James's game *Pontifuse*, whose rules section begins:

To Begin: Create a playing field as follows: From any point in the upper left-hand (northwest) quadrant of a sheet of paper, proceed one inch east and create a three-inch line bearing due south three inches. Duplicate this line one inch farther east. These are the "Lines of Versailles." Then, from the terminus of the second Line of Versailles, proceed 1.41 inches northeast and create a three-inch line bearing due west. Duplicate this line one inch farther north. These are the "Lines of the Commonwealth."

But you see, the thing is that James is kidding, because *Pontifuse* is an "alternate rules set" for the game tic-tac-toe.

There are books that tell you what words are at what reading levels. The Flesch-Kincaid Grade Level Formula is as complicated as the NFL quarterback rating, but if you learn it, you can apply it to your own text. The formula is:

grade level = 0.39 (words/sentences) + 11.8 (syllables/words) – 15.59

That'll tell you the grade level of the text you're writing. For example, that *De Bellis Antiquitatis* paragraph has a grade level of 13.22, meaning you'd need to be at least a sophomore in college to have a chance of understanding it.

You don't need a reading score test to know that obfuscation for obfuscation's sake is a bad idea. Write what people can read, and they might even play your game.

DISCARD RULES THAT CAN'T BE WRITTEN

Destroy two target nonblack creatures unless either one is a color the other isn't.

—Magic: The Gathering

That's the rules text from the *Magic* card Dead Ringers. It's about the only way it could have been written given the constraints of *Magic*'s rules. Here's why: Cards in *Magic* have one or more colors (white, blue, black, red, green). The key bit in there is "one or more." So Dracoplasm is a blue and red creature, and Horned Kavu is a green and red creature. Are they both red cards? Sure. But they're not both blue cards, and so when both are present, they're invulnerable to an effect like the one Dead Ringers has, because Dracoplasm is blue and Horned Kavu isn't. Of course, if either of them is black…

At this point, you're probably asking whether the developers of that *Magic* set ever thought, "Seriously, this is gonna make peoples' heads hurt." They did. One response to that might have been to throw out the card entirely. They didn't take that opportunity. And now James keeps a copy of Dead Ringers in his wallet to whip out at cocktail parties.

The rules you select should be chosen not on the basis of whether you like how they play, but whether you can *explain* how they play. If you can't, find some other way to play.

TAKE A BREATH

> Three important rules about industrial complexes have already been stated: (1) newly purchased units you bought at the beginning of your turn in Action 1 can be placed only in territories with industrial complexes that you have owned since the beginning of your turn; (2) newly purchased industrial complexes can be placed only in territories that you have owned since the beginning of your turn; and (3) original industrial complexes (those that you started the game with) have unlimited production—that is, you can place any number of newly purchased units on a territory with an original complex; and that new industrial complexes (those that you purchased and placed or captured during the game) have limited production per turn—that is, the number of newly purchased items that can be placed in a territory with a new complex is EQUAL to the income value of that territory.
>
> —*Axis & Allies* (1984)

That's *one* sentence. *A&A* designer Larry Harris is a genius, but that's not something I'd ever like to read again. While doing the reboot, I read that sentence over and over, and then decided that our new version of it would be fewer than 147 words.

When you write your rules, keep in mind how much your reader can read in one swoop. There's a reason why the sections of this essay are so short. I've trained myself to break up major passages into smaller sections.

It's not just comprehension that's at stake. Players often need to find a rule in a hurry, and giant blocks of text impede their ability to do so. Subheads, illustrations, occasional use of boldface, and well-timed page breaks will keep your readers on track.

GO EASY ON THE EYES

> Some Treasure cards also have a NOTORIETY value and a FAME value or
> FAME price…The six cards labeled "P1" to "P6" in red are TREASURES
> WITHIN TREASURES cards (or "T-W-T" cards) that contain other
> treasures. The CHEST (P1) is an item, but the REMAINS OF THIEF and
> MOULDY SKELETON are exchanged for items, while TOADSTOOL
> CIRCLE, CRYPT OF THE KNIGHT and ENCHANTED MEADOW are
> "Site cards"—places where treasures are located.
>
> *—Magic Realm*

At some point, *Magic Realm*'s designers decided to put all the items and
locations in all-caps. And all the spell effects. And all the values. And all the
actions. And all the encounter headings. And just about everything else. And
so they made the rulebook as irritating as a paragraph that begins most of its
sentences with "And."

Reading is harder than you think. Your eyes don't stay still; they dart about,
catching little bits here and there until, in a split second, you command them
to focus. Having all these emphasized phrases is like trying to watch six TVs
at once. You lose any sense of meaning when everything in the paragraph is
designated as THE MOST IMPORTANT THING. If it would annoy you in
an email, don't do it in your rules.

It's not just all-caps. In games I revise, I take a hard look at any term whose
first letter is capitalized. For the game *Balance of Power*, I lowercased just
about everything the designer uppercased. The term "Bonus Action" doesn't
need its capitalization; if you're taking a "bonus action," you know what it is
without the extra emphasis. But I did keep the capitalization on the names
of the pieces: Noble, King, and General. That's because it did matter to me
whether you understood the term "General action" was not the same thing as
a "general action"—that is, any old action at all.

GET YOUR FINAL VERSION PLAYTESTED

> During Step 2 of your turn, you may perform these actions in order to
> manage your holdings. These actions are: build, sprawl, remodel, reorganize,
> and gamble. You may perform any of these actions in any order, and all of
> the actions other than gamble may be performed multiple times.
>
> *—Lords of Vegas*

When James finished the final design draft of the rules for *Lords of Vegas*,
we thought we had a tight set of rules. Then they went to editing, and after
a lot of back and forth with Mayfair, we settled on a ready-to-print version.
We somehow missed the problem with the above rules paragraph, though. It's
fairly subtle, but it's also fairly disastrous.

The rules say, "you may perform these actions in order to manage your casinos." The phrase "in order to" means "so that you may"—at least that's what the people preparing the rules all thought. But "in order" also means "in the following sequence," and so after the game was released we heard from players who first built, then sprawled, then remodeled, then reorganized, then gambled. If you miss that third sentence, you're going to play the game very differently than we intended.

When you're done, get your game in the hands of a great editor. Ask Miranda Horner to help. Ask Michelle Nephew. Or Gwendolyn Kestrel, or Kim Mohan, or Sue Cook, or Darla Kennerud, or Tanis O'Connor, or any one of a dozen more brilliant game editors I can recommend.[27] They'll help you avoid a dawizard[28] that will haunt you forever. If you ever want to win an award for best rules, remember that editors like chocolate.

Also, note that the header doesn't say "Playtest your final version." By "get it playtested," I mean you should get someone who has never seen your game to play it straight from the rules. If they screw it up, you don't have a final version anymore.

The most pathetic cry for help you'll ever see is the word "final" in the file name of a rules draft. This means two things: (1) it isn't, and (2) the designer knows it isn't but really doesn't want you to notice. Sorry, designer. It's final when it's in the box.

FIX IT IN THE FAQ

Q: Why is the Underground Lake on the upper floor?
A: See, it's a special kind of levitating lake, and... All right, it's a misprint.
—FAQ for *Betrayal at House on the Hill*

Hey, if a game with my name listed as lead developer has a colossal proofreading error like this, you can forgive yourself a typo or two. Just clean it up online and in the reprint, and try not to make a habit of it. Otherwise, on this book's next printing, your game might make this list.

---

[27] They're really busy, and some of them have noncompete agreements that say they can't work on your game. But maybe one of them has a friend you could ask.

[28] A dawizard is the ultimate taboo in game editing. In a 16-page section of the 1994 *D&D* supplement *Encyclopedia Magica, Volume 1,* an editor haplessly and globally replaced all occurrences of "mage" with "wizard," leading to such epic passages as "The user may look into the ball, concentrate on any place or object, and cause the iwizard of the place or object to appear." and "The tower can absorb 200 points of dawizard before collapsing. Dawizard sustained is cumulative, and the fortress cannot be repaired (although a wish restores 10 points of dawizard sustained)." I gleefully used this story to terrify my young editors into straightening up and flying right. I never said I was a nice creative director, just a good one.

It's Not Done Till They Say It's Done

The Who, What, Where, When, and Why of Playtesting
by Teeuwynn Woodruff

I've known Tey for a quarter century, and can say that she's one of the most pleasant people you'll meet. This masks one of the cruelest streaks I've ever seen. When it comes to playtesting, she is ruthless. Where most of us feel a need to help a confused player, or just explain one little rule they're missing, Tey will let them flounder in pain, merely noting their distress on a form. She is right to do so. From decades of experience, she knows how to extract the most useful information from a playtest group, and will share that with you now. As proof of my above statements, she will start by crushing your spirit.

What I'm about to say may offend some of you reading this essay—especially those of you who have just created a shiningly perfect game that is bound to set the gaming world on fire and make you a kabillion dollars. But, please, hear me out. Your game, and possibly your wallet, will thank you for it. So, here it goes: *Your game's not as good as you think it is.* At least not until you've had people who don't hold it—or you—near and dear to their hearts play it and agree with you.

How can you make your game the best it can be? One of the most important ways, and the one most often skipped by new designers, is by playtesting it. And playtesting does not end with having your friends and family members play the game you've told them how to play. Unless you plan on including yourself in every game box, that kind of playtesting has little value.

So welcome to the who, what, where, when, and why of playtesting. We'll work our way backwards through that list. By the time we're done, you'll have a better idea of how the playtesting process works and why it's really important that you do it.

WHY SHOULD YOU PLAYTEST?

Who knows a game better than the person or people who created it? Nobody. A game is like your child. You've created it, you've seen it through challenges, and you love it. But, also just like your children, your love can blind you to your game's faults if you're not careful. And even if your game truly is brilliant, fun, and engaging, if your rules are complicated, confusing, and wrong, your audience may never even get to the point of playing your game.

A playtest can help you learn a great deal about your game's strengths and weaknesses. When you create a game, you play it, you live with it, you work with it, you become very familiar with its ins and outs. In fact, you become so familiar with it that you often become blind to the stumbling blocks others might face when they first play it. For example, in one of the many playtests we conducted to figure out the best way to teach *Magic: The Gathering* to new players, we watched as players read the rule that says you should tap your land for mana to use it. We all knew what tapping for mana meant. Everyone knows what tapping for mana means, right? Right. It means touching the land card firmly with your index finger a couple of times. D'oh. It turns out a visual reference of someone turning a card to the right and getting one of the appropriate color of mana goes a long way in teaching the game term "tap."

Playtesting is a crucial tool allowing you to step back from your game and see its flaws and strengths through new eyes—eyes of people who have never played the game before. In other words, the eyes of the consumer. Without this sort of objective playtesting, even experienced game designers can stumble on rules or gameplay elements that cause new players to give up on what is an otherwise excellent game.

WHEN SHOULD YOU PLAYTEST?

There are several different times you should consider playtesting a new game. Each type of playtest has a different goal.

A **developmental playtest** is a playtest before the rules are finalized. That sort of playtest aims at understanding if the gameplay itself is what you want. These playtests don't worry about conveying *how* to play the game; instead we're concerned only with *if* the game plays well. This first type of testing happens once you have game mechanics you're happy with. The least formal way to test is to get some people you know, tell them how to play, and see how it goes. You might start and stop several times, tinkering with the rules as you go. You can uncover some basic problems with rules and game mechanics through this method, but that's about it. You're too close to your game, and your friends and family are too close to you, to do more than this.

A **hand-taught playtest** is a better way to test how the game itself is playing. Here, you leave your friends and family behind, and recruit people in the target demographic. (Meaning the people your game is made for. And if you say "everyone," you need to start playtesting *stat*.) Then you or someone else who knows how to play hand-teaches those people how to play. Even if you are the person teaching the game (and if you have little or no budget that will probably be the case), tell the playtesters you don't have anything to do with the game's creation. Why the fib? People are more comfortable giving critical feedback to someone if they aren't worried about hurting their (meaning your) feelings.

Even if you do some good hand-taught playtesting—and I encourage you to do so—you'll want to switch to the **blind playtest** when the game is very close to finished. A blind playtest involves a number of people in the target demographic for the game, with no association to the game or its creators, playing that game as if they had just bought it at a store (or as close to that as we can make it). You should have a set of rules laid out with graphics, a mocked-up set of game components, and mocked-up packaging to put those components in. This will get you as close as possible to the "real world" of someone buying and attempting to play your game. (There's a more thorough type called a **double-blind playtest**, where even the person running the session doesn't know how to play the game.)

A final form of playtest is a **focus group playtest**. A focus group is a carefully selected group of people in your target demographic. (This may involve parents of your demographic depending on the main age of player you're going for.) A focus group can provide a lot of useful feedback on the look and feel of your product and its packaging. As with getting your rules right, getting the look and feel right will improve the odds of getting your game into the hands of the people who will love it.

Now, all these types of playtests cost money. You can spend as little as a couple pizzas and snacks, and putting your testers' names in the playtesting section of the credits. Or you can spend hundreds of thousands on complete testing including in-store product shelf-testing and the like. Since most readers of this essay are newer to game design, I won't get into how to conduct those larger-scale tests—although they give an advantage to the companies who can afford them. In the next section we'll talk about appropriate (or necessary) compensation for playtesters and other playtesting costs.

WHERE SHOULD YOU PLAYTEST?

From now on, we're going to concentrate on later-stage playtesting, because if you can only afford to do one type of playtest this is the type you should do. You have to see what reaction new people have to your game and if they can play it from the materials you're giving them.

So, where does this playtesting take place? For most games, the ideal setting for playtests is either the consumer's home or a focus group facility. People's homes are particularly good for family games or party games. Focus group facilities are great because they are neutral, the people who work at these places can recruit the playtesters using your criteria, and they provide a place for you to watch the playtests without interfering (behind a piece of one-way glass). The facility will also tape the sessions so you have records to look back on.

Of course, focus group facilities and recruitment grows costly quickly. You'll need to budget something between $5,000 and $50,000 to go this route. Getting professionals to neutrally recruit your participants and having neutral grounds to watch the playtest can reveal numerous flaws and strengths of your game, rules, and packaging. Finding out a crucial mistake in a focus group facility can make the difference between success and failure. You might discover that one of the main terms you are using in your game is offensive to a certain segment of the populace—something we saw happen at Wizards with the TCG originally named *Jyhad.*

To use a focus group facility and their recruiters, find a couple of places in your area and ask for references—particularly ones involving games and entertainment. Find out their menu of costs and determine which services you want to use. (For example, you could just choose to use their facility, or use both facility and recruiting.) For running the playtest, you should get facilitators who are familiar with the game and can ask questions after the testers play to elicit what they liked, disliked, and found hard. You should not be that person. You should be behind the mirror concentrating on the playtest. Companies usually use market researchers for this position, although focus group facilities can provide someone as well.

If you can't afford a focus group facility or your game is best tested in a home or other local environment, you'll have to go in the field to test. You can hire a market research firm to recruit testers, or you can try to do so on your own. If you recruit, get away from folks who know you. Place an ad on a college information board, ask around at after-school activity places, or get friends to post on Facebook to their friends (as long as they don't reveal they're friends with the person who made the game). The exact method depends on your pocket and who you need as playtesters.

Once you recruit playtesters and get to the location, if you are involved in the playtesting, make sure you tell the testers you had nothing to do with the game design and are just here to test it. That will help the testers feel freer to share negative as well as positive feedback.

WHAT SHOULD YOU PLAYTEST?

Alright, let's say you're at some nice family's home. They've invited you in to playtest the new family game you've been perfecting. How do you go about getting valuable and truthful information from them?

First off, be sure to bring enough playtest materials—mocked up as close to what you plan to sell as possible—for the test. If the game comes in a box, make the box. Have a set of backup materials just in case. You'll also want to bring materials to take notes, a way of videotaping the session, and post-test forms for everyone involved to fill out. (Usually these forms involve rating the gameplay, ease of learning, rules, and so on. Basically, anything you're trying to find out from the playtesters should go on that form.) Finally, you'll need a release form which gives you legal rights to use the tapes and responses for your informational purposes and swears the playtesters to secrecy until the game comes out. You can find templates for these forms online, but you may want to consider a couple of hours of legal time to draft a basic form for your company.

Hand out the release form and secrecy form, and have the playtesters sign before you begin. Children need parents to sign for them. After that is done, the facilitator hands the playtesters the box and leaves or moves away from them. The facilitator should *not* answer any questions about the game or game materials while the testers play—or attempt to play. And neither should you or anyone else there. This is not the time to defend your game or correct mistakes. Seeing where people stumble over rules, mechanics, and visuals is what you're here for. So be quiet! (If you're conducting a developmental playtest, you will tell the players how to play and correct any play mistakes, but don't comment on the game itself.)

Once the playtest is done (either in a given time frame or until the playtesters have completed the game), pass out the post-playtest sheets. Once testers fill out this sheet, the facilitator (and possibly others) should ask testers questions about what they liked and didn't like about the game, as well as what they found problematic and anything that helped them understand the game better. If you saw places the testers played wrong, make sure to tell them the correct way to play and find out what led them to the error. Some errors are matters of omission. For example, when playtesting a new soccer TCG in England, we found that simply telling kids to draw a hand of cards wasn't enough—that led to players picking up their entire decks! We had to be more specific—shuffle your deck, put it down, and draw seven cards off the top. But many errors come down to poor formatting, poor—or no—graphics, poor or missing examples of play, and rambling text. Nobody likes to read rules, so your goal is to get the game across correctly with as few words as possible. If you can say it with a picture, do so.

Finally, pay the playtesters their consideration (often $25-$100 each) if you are doing so. And make sure you note their names correctly for inclusion in the credits.

After the playtest is over, go back and rework the game—then playtest again. Ideally, you'll have a set of very clean playtests, where the players enjoy themselves and learn from the rules, before shipping the game.

When testing, try to have three to twelve different groups play your game. Very often, you will find one or two groups that do something or play in a way that's very different from most people. Having a larger pool of playtesters helps you find out more consistently where the current strengths and weaknesses of your game lay.

WHO SHOULD YOU PLAYTEST WITH?

You should playtest with people in the target demographic of your game. Is your game aimed at 6- to 8-year-old boys? Then get them in for playtests. Do you have an adult party game? Have a playtest with friends in one of their homes and see how it goes. Does your game contain an electronic device? Then be sure you have the devices you need with the game loaded for testers. (If the technical elements of the game aren't ready yet then you'll want a series of "screen" pages. The testers show the facilitator which "button" they are pushing and the facilitator hands out the next "screen.")

If you don't playtest with the people your game is targeted at, the playtests won't help much. And remember, if you're playtesting with children, you'll want to get the parents' feedback too—after all, they'll probably be the ones buying the game.

So, you have your demographics and you've got materials for the testers ready to go. Time to recruit the testing troops! You can recruit from places your ideal demographic are likely to be. If girls 7 to 10 is your target, you may want to approach after school activity locations, sports games, the library, and the like. For college students who like sports, post information near the sports parts of the campus, try to get in their newspaper or online information page—and be sure to tell them who matches your criteria and how much you will pay them right off the start.

Getting playtesters for your game wouldn't be too difficult if all you needed was warm bodies. The issue is getting testers in the proper demographic who are outgoing, articulate, and analytically minded enough to express any problems they are having with game…. Yeah, all that's true. But going beyond the niceties, you really have to determine if someone is open to directly criticizing the work—as harshly as they feel it merits. Also, you'll probably want some players who get pleasure from breaking the game. They play by searching for loopholes and amorphous rules they can use to their advantage—often pissing off the other players—but just as often showing you some major problems you need to fix before debuting your game.

In order to find a solid array of playtesters who have the characteristics you want, you'll have to conduct demographic surveys. These surveys ask basic information about the person. But for a game test, you'll likely want to know things like: What games do you play? How often do you play? What game is your favorite and why? What makes you pick up a game at a store? What can make you give up on a game?

In your post-playtest survey, in addition to quizzing the testers about specific aspects of your game and your rules, ask the testers to name their favorite games again. Also, ask how likely they are to purchase the game (1/2/3/4/5 scale).

I could write a book on the ins and outs of playtesting, but probably the most important thing to remember is to *stay neutral*. If the testers know it's your game or if you sit across from them rolling your eyes or making verbal comments, your data is tainted. And that won't do your "baby" any good when it's time to kick the game out on its own in the real world!

Teeuwynn Woodruff *is a game, puzzle, and events designer in Sammamish, Washington. At Wizards of the Coast, Teeuwynn worked on games like Dungeons & Dragons, Magic: The Gathering, Pokémon, Harrow, Betrayal at House on the Hill, and Duelmasters. Her puzzles appear in magazines such as Games and Wired, as well as in alternate reality games. As creative director for Lone Shark Games, she has created games and immersive events for companies such as Microsoft, Sony, Lucasfilm, Turbine, ArenaNet, and Southpeak Interactive. She can't even count the number of hours she's spent watching playtests of all kinds.*

Part 4
Presentation

In which we clean our games up and get them ready to leave the house, with hopes they will return will lots of new friends.

Amazing Errors in Prototyping

by Steve Jackson

The phrase "Steve Jackson games" (lowercase "g") defines two things: games designed by Steve Jackson, and games published by Steve Jackson Games. Those two sets are not coterminous, but there are a whole lot of games in both. Steve has made and reviewed more prototypes than just about anyone, and oh my lord, the stories he tells…well, they're right here. There are many ways to make good prototypes. Read on for the ways to fail spectacularly at that goal.

You may hope to sell your game to a publisher. You may already have a publisher…you may already be a publisher…and you now hope to sell a great number of copies to hobby distributors or chain stores. Either way, you know that it would be a mistake to send your game to press, fill your garage with shipping cartons, and then start marketing the game using actual samples.

Ahh….You do know that, right?

A prototype is an advance copy of a game, created before the game goes to press. Prototypes may be "working," intended for evaluation by playtesters and potential publishers, or they may be "display" prototypes, with finished art and components, intended for the eyes of distributors or chain buyers. Some display prototypes have beautiful covers, boards, and components, but the rulebook is unfinished or absent. The buyers at Toy Fair want to see your meeples, but they don't care about your rules! The publishers displaying these prototypes may not even have designed the game yet! If the concept (a licensed property, perhaps) and graphics attract interest, then they'll create a game…

This essay deals with working prototypes, because that's what I know best. If you want to make your working prototype beautiful as well, more power to you. At conventions like the appropriately named Protospiel[29], one may see amateur[30] prototypes that look like real, finished, professionally published

---

[29] Protospiel (www.protospiel.org) is, to quote the website, "annual get-together of amateur and established game designers to test and promote nearly-finished game prototypes." There is now a Southern spinoff, Protospiel South (www.protospielsouth.com).

[30] I use amateur, not in the modern and condescending sense, but in the original meaning of "one who does a thing for the love of it rather than for money." An amateur can display as much skill and commitment as any professional; for instance, most Olympic athletes are amateurs. In game design, amateurs may be able to spend less time per week than professionals, but they are unhindered by deadlines, and the results can be remarkable.

games. But to present a game to a publisher, you don't need a beautiful prototype. You just need a clear, playable one.

I have seen some prototypes that were not good, and now we reach the meat of the essay. As you read, you will laugh, but my goal is not to make you laugh. My goal is to reduce the odds that you will do these things, because if you do, your perfectly clever game may languish forever in obscurity.

LESS IS MORE

The designer was concerned that we would object to the number of counters in his game, so he sent a prototype with fewer counters. The shortage of pieces made the game unfinishable.

Yes, it was annoying that we could not finish the game without supplying a few more bits. But that was not the deal-killer. We're a game company; we have lots of game pieces around. The deal-killer was that it first seemed that the designer didn't understand his own game...and, when we heard his reasoning, it was obvious that he was trying to psych us. He was withholding information about the gameplay from his potential publisher! No, thank you.

MORE IS LESS

The designer specified that the game worked for 2 to 8 players, and sent setup rules and components enough for an 8-player game. It turned out that all his games had been with 3, 4, or 5 players. Never once had it been tried with 2 players, or with more than 5.

Again, the designer was withholding information...in this case, he was making claims not backed up by playtesting. Ironically, for us, 3 to 5 players is the sweet spot. If he had started by saying "It works for 3 to 5, and might work for more, but I have not tested it with more than 5," we would have thought that quite reasonable.

ANACHRONISTIC COMPONENTS

The designer had created new cards based on his own last round of playtesting, but the rules had not been updated to match the new cards, leading to utter confusion on the part of the people who played it in our office.

This told us that the designer was sloppy, and called into question his claim to have extensively playtested his game. Whenever you revise one component of the game, you should review your other components to see if they need updating.

HEY, LET'S PUT IN ELEPHANTS! ELEPHANTS ARE COOL!

The designer had some great ideas for new cards (or so he thought) and added them after his last playtest, and then sent us the untested cards.

This is really just another way to make the same mistake. If you represent to the publisher that the game is tested, make sure it's all tested. In this particular case, if the designer had included a separate packet labeled "Do Not Open This Unless You've Played the Game and Liked It," and explained what he was doing, we would not have objected. As it was, he waited for us to point out problem cards, and then explained, "Oh, I didn't test those!" We were not amused.[31]

IF A THING IS WORTH DOING, IT'S WORTH OVERDOING

The designer paid a professional artist to illustrate the cards for his prototype.

We've actually seen this more than once. It becomes a problem when we really hate the illustrator's style. Had the designer done the best he could and submitted playable components built with desktop publishing, we would have been free to imagine whatever graphics we thought best. His prototype drew more attention to the (bad) art than to the design. And in one case, the cover letter made it clear that the designer really liked the (bad) art and expected the publisher to reimburse him for the (high) art expenses and use the (bad) art!

Of course, this can work both ways. Twice, I have bought designer-illustrated games because the art really grabbed me. Of course, neither of those games has yet seen print; there may be a moral here.

I CAN PLAY THIS WITH MY EYES CLOSED

The designer playtested his game with wooden blocks, but saved money by sending us flat semi-transparent counters, which got lost on his boldly and jaggedly colored map. He was then surprised that we had trouble playing.

Another designer sent three types of cards, intended to be different decks, but indistinguishable when turned upside-down.

"Working prototype" means it works. Make it easy to use. There's a reason that Kinko's carries several colors of cardstock.

THIS IS SO WRONG IT CANNOT BE SUMMARIZED IN A SINGLE CUTE SUBHEAD

The designer decided the setup instructions should be modified, so he edited his map in squiggly ballpoint pen before sending it to us. Sadly, we could not read his handwriting!

Where do I start? Just don't do this. Don't do anything like this. If you are so sheltered and/or self-centered that you cannot realize that someone else might not be able to make out your squiggles, you should not be trying to write rules

[31] Yes, I am well aware of *We Didn't Playtest This At All*. It is a work of genius, a thing of beauty, an achievement for the ages, a clever deconstruction of the game designer's art and craft, and now it's been done. Find your own shtick.

for other people to play. You should become one of these guys who spends 20 years writing complex rules for a game that nobody else will ever see.

FEDERAL EXPRESS LOVES YOU BUT WE DO NOT

A designer shipped us a prototype in which the game boards (plural) had all been laminated to half-inch hardwood planks.

Another designer shipped us a tiny cardboard pack of cards packed in a huge annoying carton of peanuts.

This really illustrates how subjective the evaluation process can be. Neither of the above examples made it any harder for us to play (at least, once we cleaned all the peanuts off the table). But both of them left us saying "What is this guy thinking?" In general, you don't want to leave your publisher thinking, before he even tries your game, that you are some kind of nut.[32]

OR HE COULD HAVE WRITTEN ANOTHER THOUSAND WORDS

The designer appended a note to the rules saying, "Some illustrations would be useful here."

Yes. Yes, they would. Quite useful. In this case, they would probably have gotten us to try the game at least once. And perhaps before he submitted it elsewhere, he created those illustrations. I am mildly curious as to whether he included this note because his playtesters asked for illustrations, but I wasn't curious enough to ask.

THE MORAL OF THE STORY

All of this boils down to:

- A working prototype must include everything it actually takes to play the game.
- A working prototype must not include anything you have not tested thoroughly.
- A working prototype should be about gameplay. Don't try to dictate the art or the marketing!
- Above all, and summarizing everything else: A working prototype must be playable, legible, and user-friendly.

Steve Jackson is the founder and president of the uncreatively-named Steve Jackson Games. His designs include Ogre, Car Wars, Illuminati, GURPS, Munchkin, and Zombie Dice. He intends to retire from his ill-gotten Munchkin gains, and keep right on creating games. He waves off all insinuations that this is not "retirement."

---

[32] That's my shtick, and it's taken.

Everything You Always Wanted to Know About Prototypes*

(But Were Afraid to Ask)

by Dale Yu

*Now that you've read Steve Jackson's essay on what **not** to do with your prototypes, here's Dale again to tell you what you **should** do. Dale, who's known as "The Gaming Doctor" both because of his medical practice and because of his ability to fix games, spends a lot of time looking at prototypes. I've asked him to adapt a nuts and bolts essay he wrote for boardgamenews.com on prototypes, because it tells you quite a bit about how to put your game's best foot forward.*

For better or for worse, I've come into contact with a lot of prototypes over the past two years. I've designed a few games of my own, and struggled with how to make a quality prototype that would appeal to others without taking too much time and effort on my part. My error was trying to cut corners on my prototypes—I now believe that you cannot spend too much time or effort on your prototype. I've evaluated many games for companies to see whether those games were viable for development and eventual production. I'd like to spend a bit of time talking what makes me think a prototype looks good.

THE FIRST IMPRESSION

This shouldn't come as a surprise, but with prototypes, first impressions are important. Having been on the "industry" side in the past few years, oftentimes the first view of the prototype really influences my opinion of the game. If you have only 20 or 30 minutes to show someone a game and convince them of its greatness, you'd like to have as many positive things as possible and limit the negatives.

So, what's important to me when I first see a prototype? For me, the most important thing is the overall appearance. I like prototypes to look clean and well-made. I'd like the box art and text to look nice, and when I open the box, I'd like to see the bits organized nicely. If it looks like you've spent a lot of time making your prototype, that goes a long way to impress me. Art is less important for me (as I know that I can't draw a thing), but others I've talked to also appreciate it when there are nice graphics already integrated into the prototype.

RULES AND MANIFEST

After the initial appearance, it's important to make sure that the rules are well written and easy to understand. Of course, if you're showing your game to someone, it's easy to give a detailed description of the game and answer any questions. However, if you're not around to explain, you need to make sure that the person reading the rules can understand how to play the game. If you show a game to a game company, and there is interest, you may be asked to leave a copy with them (or you may have mailed the copy of the game to the publisher). So you can count on someone eventually seeing your game cold, and they'll need to approach the game from the rules alone. I'd recommend that you add in extra rules and clarifications where possible to answer as many questions as you can. I wouldn't worry about writing the most succinct set of rules at this point—if the game gets picked up, there will be a technical writer somewhere along the line who will edit the rules for you.

There are other little things that help me learn a game from the rules alone. First, it helps to have pictures or diagrams of important or confusing parts of the game, especially for setup. Also, it's helpful to have a manifest of bits. For many Eurogames, there are all sorts of counters, little wooden cubes, and whatnot used in any game. While you may clearly understand that the 3mm blue wooden cubes obviously represent fish and the yellow plastic disks are obviously dolphins, it's often difficult for me to discern what bits are what when I don't know the game. If I have to spend 20 minutes figuring out how things go together, it doesn't get the game off to a good start.

Next, make sure the rules are correct! I understand that prototypes are always currently being revised, but make sure that the rules reflect the current components that are in the box! If you don't take enough time to update your prototype, it certainly leaves a negative impression on me. I would recommend that you leave a way for people to get in touch with you in the rules or on the box. I have had a number of prototypes come through my game group (from different publishers)—but I had no way to contact the game designer to ask them rules questions. Don't assume that your contact information will be passed on when the prototype is evaluated by different people!

COMPONENTS

Now let me switch gears a bit and talk about actual prototype construction. I've managed to collect a lot of things that help me make prototypes at home (or improve upon prototypes that I receive). Here's what I usually use:

Cards

Cards are found in most Eurogames, and it helps to have a bunch of different cards around to use. The two most commonly used cards for me are 1) old *Magic: The Gathering* commons and 2) Bicycle playing cards (both red and blue). Years ago, I was a serious *Magic* player, and I had about 10,000 extra cards lying around at one point. *Magic* cards are useful to have around as they have a uniform back and they are plentiful (at least in my house). The Bicycle cards are extras from the US Playing Card Company store (located here in Cincinnati). These also have uniform backs and can be easily pasted up. I've got literally hundreds of decks of playing cards.

I also keep old business cards. I still have the last three or four iterations of my personal business card—when they have to be replaced, I simply keep the old ones. I find that they work well for initial prototypes. You can handwrite stuff on the empty "card backs," and they all conveniently have the same information on the other side.

Finally, I make a point of keeping extra cards from old games or from thrift-store specials. It's much rarer that I'll find a use for these cards, but you never know. I like to always have around an extra copy of *Rage* (the Amigo card game, not the White Wolf CCG). This little gem has cards numbered 0 thru 15 in six different colors. This comes in handy for all sorts of purposes. While my stash is dwindling, I think I still have two copies left around to be plundered for prototypes.

Card sleeves

If you have cards in your prototype, you have a few ways to get the information on the card. The easiest way is to print up a proxy on a piece of paper and then slip it into a card sleeve. If you need to shuffle the cards, you can always put a card in the sleeve as well to give it some heft.

I use two different types of sleeves. The first is the "penny sleeve," which is a ridiculously thin, cellophane-like sleeve. They are called penny sleeves because they are often found in packs of 100 for about a dollar. They aren't the most durable sleeves, but they're cheap and can be useful if you have a lot of things to sleeve. The other type I'll often use is the Ultra Pro sleeve. These are much more expensive, about 5 cents per sleeve, but they are much more durable. They also come in a variety of colors. I think that I have bits and pieces of eight different colors in the prototype closet right now. I find that the best way to buy these is find dealers at trade shows and game conventions, and buy the colors they can't usually sell. They might be ugly, but I have 2,500 matching purple sleeves for my *Dominion* prototype that I bought for $30.

Stickers

Stickers are nice for re-labeling things and allowing you to reuse a lot of components. I keep a number of different sticker types around:

- Full page stickers—these are for printing large scale work like boards.
- Name badge stickers—these stickers are just the right size for *Magic* cards.
- Removable Avery address labels—these let you edit things on the fly.

Paper

You will burn through a lot of paper. Most of the paper that we keep at home is either used for work or for my wife's Sunday School classes, but I have access to it all when I need! Here is what I've got in the closet right now (the pound sign refers to weight—the higher the number, the thicker the paper):

- 20# letter and legal white copy paper
- 24# 11×17 ledger paper
- 28# super-bright HP laser printer paper
- 32# Astrobrights in pink, green, yellow, teal, purple
- 20# Staples house brand paper in yellow, green, and light blue
- 24# Office Depot pastels
- Construction paper
- 110# white card stock
- 110# assorted pastel card stock
- 67# gray card stock photo paper
- Inkjet iron-on transfer paper

Bits

Though I usually wouldn't admit it, I've been known to throw out games. Most of those are crap that I picked up at thrift stores thinking that they would someday get played. Others are games that are inexplicably incomplete (and I didn't like them anyways). Before I throw them out, I raid the box for any loose wooden or plastic bits. I also save any play money or cards. I've got a fairly sizable tackle box of bits that I keep in the back of the basement. It comes in handy when I need a replacement piece for a game, and it gives me a wide selection of bits to use when I'm trying to cobble together a prototype.

The other important thing to keep around are extra boards. Finding material that is suitable to be used as a board is hard to come by for me. So, I keep a stack of extra boards lying around. If I can, I'll just print up stuff on full sheet sticker paper and slap it on the extra boards that I have lying around.

Dice are also very handy to have around. They can be used for all sorts of things. I usually have everything from d4 to d20 lying around in various colors. I also have a few blocks of small Chessex 6-siders in at least six colors, as it seems that d6 are needed most often.

The other prototype gaming bit that has been helpful to have around are the plastic cubes and transparent chips that can be had at most teacher's supply stores. Eurogames seem to have lots of cubes and things that need to be marked. The variety that I buy usually has eight or ten different colors, so there's generally enough variety for any game that I need to make.

There are lots of online retailers that sell gaming bits in various shapes and sizes, among them Spiele Materiele, Meeple Source, the Game Crafter, and many others.

Bags and baggies

I have a nice stash of Crown Royal bags in the basement, given to me by a bartender friend. I also have an assortment of plastic baggies of varying sizes and shapes. Of course, the cheapest ones are the Ziploc sandwich- and snack-size bags that work for most things. I also have bags in sizes such as 2"×3", 3"×4", and 3"×5" from Uline or Associatedbag.com. I tend to be a bagger of bits in my normal games, so it comes as no surprise that I also bag up everything in my prototypes.

Boxes

I try to use new clean boxes. The Container Store has white sturdy boxes of all sizes and shapes. I've also been known to reuse boxes of discarded games, especially the Kosmos 2-player square boxes. If I reuse boxes, I print up full sheet labels to paste up all the sides of the box, so that there is no confusion as to what is in the box.

HARDWARE

OK, I'll admit that I'm a bit lucky in this regard. Both my wife and I have occasion to work out of the house, and as a result we've got a lot of office equipment around.

Color laser printer and copier

As far as making game components goes, the HP 2840 Laserprinter/Copier/Fax has been a godsend. Having a color printer and color copier has greatly improved the quality of my prototypes/homebrews. It also has the ability to print on transparencies which has helped with some prototypes.

Computer

If you've got a printer, that also means that you've likely got a computer hooked up to it. I have found it essential to have Adobe Photoshop or GIMP around in order to manipulate images to help my prototypes look good. A clip art CD or online subscription to clipart.com (or even Google image searching) is also a vital tool in making things look their best.

Laminator

I have a nice little pouch laminator that I can use to make cards, player mats, and all sorts of other things. The laminated bits can be used with dry-erase markers nicely. My laminator is 11.5 inches wide so it can accommodate letter-sized paper.

THE FINAL IMPRESSION

Finally, if you'd really like people to take a good look at the game, make sure you send them (or leave them with) at least one fully playable copy of the game. Promising to send someone the rules to a game and a full set of graphics to allow them to assemble a game isn't good enough. Remember, you're the one trying to sell your game. If it takes someone else a lot of time and hassle to put together a prototype of an untested game, it's simply not going to happen—especially if you've been exposed to as many awful prototypes as I have. Yes, I realize that this might be expensive and time consuming, but if you want folks to take a look at your prototype, it's going to be worth it to you to make it look as good as you can and have it ready to play right out of the box.

Life's a Pitch

How to License Your Game
by Richard C. Levy

If you want your games to sell thousands of copies, you can get some great advice at game convention seminars. But if you want your games to sell millions of copies, you probably should listen to Richard Levy. He's a master of the mass market, and in this essay, he shares some tips about how to pitch your game to the big boys and girls. As he notes, "The capacity for creating is shared in measure by everyone. The capacity for selling is known but to a few."

A new game is a delicate thing. To borrow a thought from the Roman poet Ovid, it can be killed by a sneer or a yawn; it can be stabbed to death by a quip and worried to death by a frown on the right marketing executive's brow.

Before you can present your game to a potential publisher (what the mass market calls a "licensee"), you must get through the door. This action, by its high visibility, becomes a vital part of your presentation.

Chances are you are unknown to the company. You are, therefore, untested. Introduce yourself correctly and you will be welcomed. Do it the wrong way and it could haunt you. Not unlike game design, getting through the door requires imagination, knowledge, and the ability to think of future moves before playing them.

BE PREPARED

Before you approach a company, do your homework. As in sports, you'll play as you practice. Nothing beats good preparation. There is no substitute for it. Know your game and the history of its category. Know the market. Know what your game will cost to make. Know how to sell the vision for your game. Most of all, know that getting a licensee or publisher for your game is not going to be easy.

INFORMATION IS POWER

Beyond what you can find out about a company on the internet, talk to other inventors that have licensed games to your preferred company and see how they found the experience. Nothing beats empirical feedback from a licensor, satisfied or otherwise. If you do not know an inventor that has worked with a company you would like to pitch, ask the company for references. Most game companies will share the names of their inventors. If you find resistance to such a simple request, I'd take that as a sign to go elsewhere.

Learn the strengths and interests of the companies you target. These will vary especially between specialty and mass market companies.

SELL YOURSELF FIRST

You are selling two things, yourself and your game. It is during this initial stage that you set the tone for further discussions. First impressions are lasting impressions. Images are engraved into psyches. Conduct yourself well the first time, and you'll be welcome any time. I cannot stress the importance of being able to make an encore because ninety-nine percent of what I license happens after Act III, if not even later than that.

ON TAKING REJECTION

I take rejections as rehearsals before big events. To me a "no" means "not now." My biggest games have been rejected by multiple companies. *Adverteasing*, for example, was rejected by Milton Bradley, Parker Brothers, and too many other game publishers to list. Then a year and a half after I started to pitch it under the working trademark *Ad Infinitum*, Cadaco, a small game publisher in Chicago, licensed my adult social interactive game and sold over one million copies. In 2011, the 25th anniversary edition of *Adverteasing* was released.

Do not let rejection shake your confidence. My experience is that products get better the more times they are presented. Rejection can be positive if you turn it into constructive growth. Unless someone points out a fatal flaw, I tend to stay the course.

EGO CONTROL

Creative and inventive people hate to be rejected or criticized. They are typically extremely defensive where their creations are concerned.

An out-of-control ego can kill deals. While you need a healthy ego to serve as body armor, an unruly ego can change to arrogance if not governed. Great mistakes are made when we feel we are beyond questioning.

It is the cross-pollination and subsequent collaboration of external forces and ideas on my games that result in success—success in which many parties share.

BEATING THE ODDS

It is important that your expectations be realistic. The odds you are up against are staggering. In an attempt to keep things real, let's look at the competition for a slot within a company's line. Since my experience is greater with mass market game publishers than with specialty publishers, here is what it looks like inside Hasbro in a typical year, per Mike Hirtle, Hasbro's vice president of inventor relations and product acquisition. These numbers do not take into account the concepts that may be generated internally.

- 1,300 external game concepts submitted per year
- 300 brought in house
- 150 presented to Marketing
- 25–30 optioned or licensed
- 10–15 taken to market
- 3–4 successes
- 1–2 BIG successes

If you don't find these numbers sobering, go back to Start.

THE SELLING SEASON

For every rule of when to sell, there is a story that proves it wrong. I, therefore, think the perfect time to pitch an idea is whenever a company wants to listen. Strike while the proverbial iron is hot. Don't hesitate. Every company marches to its own cadence.

This having been said, there are sales cycles as well as product review sessions. You should know when the company makes its presentations to the trade and conducts internal test reviews.

MULTIPLE SUBMISSIONS

If you have more than one prototype, and the situation merits, you should consider making multiple submissions to different companies. I would not be shy about doing this given the prolonged time frame companies take these days to make decisions (read: the paralysis of analysis). I make this decision on a case by case basis. The decision is made easier for me if my game is covered by a patent or a trademark.

If a company asks that you hold off further presentations until it has had an opportunity to review the game, set guidelines. In all fairness to the company, some games require a reasonable number of days to be properly considered. However, if you feel the company is over-reaching, seek some earnest money to hold the game out of circulation. The amount of time and money is negotiable. Also, during any hold period, insist that the submission not be shown to anyone outside the company such as trade buyers.

There is a value to multiple submissions that goes beyond having the game reviewed faster and by more companies. A multiple submission can set up a bidding war for the game. I have had this happen on occasion. It is an understood tactic of negotiation. Do not be timid about suggesting it.

INVENTION MARKETING COMPANIES

My rule is simple. Never deal with invention marketing firms, patent trolls, or agents that reach you through TV, radio, newspaper, magazine ads, unsolicited direct mail appeals, or email. It is as simple as that. No ifs, ands, or buts. Here is the best way to remember this advice: Ad equals bad.

Mark A. Spikell, co-founder of the Entrepreneurship Center at the School of Business Administration of George Mason University says that about 80 percent of the people claiming to help inventors build a business, market their product, or raise capital are conmen, beggars, thieves, and/or incompetents.

LEGITIMATE AGENTS

If you decide to use the services of an agent or broker, make sure that the person has a track record of success in the game category. Ask for references. Make sure you speak to no less than three satisfied inventor clients.

Many game publishers will give you the names of agents with whom they work. Mattel and Hasbro, for example, distribute such listings.

If the agent asks you to sign a representation agreement, make sure that it is not too broad in scope, especially on the first deal. It is prudent to make a first agreement for one product only until you see how things work out.

Be comfortable with the length of time the agent wants to tie your game up. Know exactly what rights you are handing over to the agent in terms of the scope of representation. And perhaps more important than anything is your ability to get out of the agreement should the agent not give you his or her best efforts.

If an agent asks for up-front money, I would run, not walk, to the next candidate on your list. Further, be careful of agents that charge for evaluations. The best and most successful agents take their percentage of advances and royalties, and do not work on a fee basis. Agents typically get between a third and half of a deal.

It benefits you to be a party to any deal the agent makes. Game publishers have no problem cutting two checks, one to the inventor and one to the agent. You never want anyone between you and your money source. You never want to give contract signing authority to an agent. Make sure that you always know what you are getting into.

Lastly, be sure that you comprehend how the agent is handling the confidentiality of your game, what the agent warrants, indemnifies, and so forth.

PROTOTYPES

I always try to present a looks-like/works-like prototype of a game. That's a three-dimensional model that functions exactly like the production model, although it need not be made from production materials.

In my experience, nothing beats ThomasNet for one-stop shopping when you are looking for components. ThomasNet lists more than 600,000 industrial companies in North America, indexed by more than 60,000 product and service categories. You'll find them on-line at www.thomasnet.com.

BRAND POWER

Do not underestimate or overlook the value that a well known trademark can add to your game. High visibility trademarks create instant recognition which, ipso facto, requires less investment from the publisher to make the game known. Strong brand equity also influences the trade when it comes to deciding which new games to purchase for sale in their stores. Jeff Chester, executive director of the Center for Digital Democracy calls this trend the "brandwashing" of America.

There are well-known trademarks that come free of charge because they are in the public domain, such as literary classics. Other trademarks will require a royalty.

Early in my career, companies looked for new and creative names like *Adverteasing* to put on games. But for the past two decades, I have worked very hard to marry my games to strong, well-known brands. Some examples of such games are: *Men Are from Mars, Women Are from Venus: The Game* (Mattel), *Chicken Soup for the Soul: The Game* (Cardinal Games), *Magnetic Poetry* (Magnetic Poetry, Inc.), and *Warner Bros. Trivial Pursuit* (Hasbro).

Each of these games has its own interesting backstory. But let's look at *Men Are from Mars, Women Are from Venus* as a template for fusing a brand and an idea. The game was based on the book of the same name. I tracked down the book's author, John Gray, through his publisher, and gave him a call. I pitched John to allow me to put his brand on a social interactive game, a category of games in which I have specialized and had success. We would create the game and he would have input and total approval. We struck a deal. He agreed. Then I went to Mattel. The company loved the idea. Our game sold over 1 million copies the first year.

Chicken Soup for the Soul also started with a phone call to an author. We created several games for this brand. They had combined sales of more than 750,000 copies.

Coffee Talk, released by Pressman, is based on a well-known pop culture term. In this case, we applied for the *Coffee Talk* trademark at the U.S. Patent and Trademark Office and will control it ourselves. We presented the game packaged in a coffee pouch. It was the combination of the trademark and package that made the game irresistible to Pressman.

When negotiating for trademarks, remember that pigs get fat, hogs get slaughtered. If combining your game with a strong trademark will increase the odds of success, run the numbers. Would you rather have a smaller percentage of a game that sells big numbers or a larger piece of a game that is lost in the clutter of board game jungle?

In conclusion

It is a misconception if you think there is an easy dollar to be made creating and licensing games. In an industry filled with the legends of instant millionaires such as *Pictionary*'s Robert Angel and *Trivial Pursuit*'s Chris Haney and Scott Abbott, few game inventors make a lot of money. Most game inventors toil day in and day out for little or no reward. In this way, game inventing is on par with the most highly competitive businesses. This having been said, the game business has an insatiable appetite for new product and it remains a fertile frontier for the independent game inventor. I can attest to this fact.

Richard C. Levy *is a 35-year veteran game inventor with a flair for marketing. He co-authored* The Toy & Game Inventor's Handbook *and authored* The Complete Idiot's Guide to Cashing In on Your Inventions. *His designs include the games* Noteability, Adverteasing, Coffee Talk, Chicken Soup for the Soul: The Game, *and* Men Are from Mars, Women Are from Venus: The Game, *as well as the co-development of the worldwide smash animatronic toy* Furby, *which has sold 60 million units to date.*

Getting Your Game Published

The Process from Proposal to Print
by Michelle Nephew

I'm ending this book with an epic-length essay on publication by Michelle Nephew. Michelle is the nicest but most brutal critic you will ever have in the game industry, if you're that lucky. As the "tenured editor" at Atlas Games, Michelle's job is to figure out which games Atlas will make and what they will look like when they do. She once told me that for her to publish a game, she would have to want to demo it for the rest of her life. Now that's pressure. I dare you to pitch her a game without reading this article and taking her advice to heart. Actually, I'd probably bring popcorn.

Everyone has an idea for a game that they're working on, whether it's a board game they made for their kids, or a card game variant they thought up with their buddies. But actually getting your game professionally published is a lot harder than coming up with that original idea. Knowing how game submission and development works can give you a leg up on all the other freelance game designers out there, and prepare you for your part in the process.

Sure, you could go another route, like self-publishing. But many beginning game designers have full-time jobs and families. They have other things to do besides—and very little experience with—the things that publishers take care of. And they're often short on cash. When you license your idea to a publisher, they're are the ones who pay for everything. They pay you for your idea, their staff develops your game idea with playtesting and editing, they hire artists to illustrate it and graphic designers to put all the pieces together into a professional-looking package ready for press, and they pay a printer to actually manufacture the game. Then they spend more money to advertise and market your game, and they take care of warehousing and fulfillment—selling and shipping your game to their distributors, who then in turn sell it to retailers.

That's a pretty good deal for most people. But that said, it's very hard for an independent designer to get a foot in the door with the giant, mass-market game companies like Hasbro and Mattel. They put up a lot of hurdles for inexperienced designers, like requiring you to have an agent to represent you, and there are only about a dozen of these that they'll deal with. They won't take meetings with individual game designers.

But there are publishers out there who are a bit easier to approach about your game—small to mid-sized publishers in the hobby games industry. These are the folks whose games you generally won't find at Target or Walmart, but rather at your friendly local games store.

CHOOSING YOUR PUBLISHER

The first step to getting your game published—after actually designing the game, of course—is to submit your idea to some publishers. This is a task that doesn't benefit from a scatter-shot approach. Sending out unsolicited letters to every publisher whose address you can find on the internet is just going to get them all thrown out unopened. And if you actually send a prototype of your game with it, that's a lot of investment in postage and materials to see hit the trash bin. The entirely preventable reason for this inevitable outcome is a sad lack of targeting and background research on the people you're approaching.

Most publishers who are accepting submissions from the general public post their submission policy on their website. This is because they require certain things from submissions, like a signed release form without which they can't even look at your idea. This form usually just says that the publisher isn't obligated to publish your game because they accept your submission for review, it warns you that they may already be working on a similar idea to yours that they can't necessarily tell you about, and it asks you to verify that you own all the rights to your idea and that it hasn't been published before. Unfortunately, ideas are a dime a dozen, and not copyrightable. Game rules themselves are also not copyrightable; only their specific expression is. That's why some new designers worry that a publisher will steal their idea, and so they get unnecessarily skittish about release forms. Most publishers, though, are in business because they want to publish quality games, and they're accepting submissions because they want to find new designers to work with. They'd much rather pay you for your idea than steal it, because that's really a very small part of the overall budget for producing and marketing a new game, after all. But they need to protect themselves legally, and won't look at your submission without a release.

Even if you find a publisher who's currently accepting game proposals, and you find their submission policy and release form online, it's still not always a good idea to invest your time in actually submitting your idea to them. The reason is that every publisher has a different corporate identity—they're known for publishing a certain kind of game. If your game is an edgy, surreal streetfighting card game, sending it to someone who specializes in WWII miniatures games isn't going to get you anywhere. It's a much better idea to target your submissions to game companies who offer complementary, but not identical, games to what you've come up with. Go to your friendly local games store and find half a dozen games that are similar to yours, then write down the names of their publishers so you can try sending your proposal to them.

You'll get a lot farther with a publisher who's already shown an interest in the type of game you've created.

WHAT PUBLISHERS LOOK FOR

Publishers are professionals, and want to work with professionals. Your job in submitting a proposal is to show that you're a professional, and that working with you will go smoothly for your publisher. Prove that you're a designer who can follow instructions, meet deadlines, and produce easily published work. While a well-assembled proposal may not guarantee these qualities, a haphazard submission tells them that you're not ready for professional work. So make sure your proposal is neat and organized. Always double-check for inaccurate information, incorrect addresses, misspellings, and other mistakes before you put it in the mail. And be sure your proposal displays a solid understanding of the game system you're working with, especially if this is a supplement to an existing game.

Beyond professionalism, publishers look for a variety of things in new games. A good number of those are discussed here, but remember that every publisher emphasizes some of these points over others. A game that a publisher chooses to publish probably won't hit every single one of these criteria, but will likely fit several of them especially well. A good game should have:

The fun factor: First and foremost, the game should be fun. "Fun" means different things to everyone, but publishers know it when they see it and so should you.

Player interaction: This is a big part of your fun factor. Players should affect other players whenever possible, not interact only with their own game pieces. And games that encourage table talk are more fun than those conducted in silence.

Immediacy of play: Minimizing set-up time and designing short rules lets players get into game play quickly and start having fun right away. But even if your game is a six-hour strategy game, make sure it has as little downtime as possible, minimizes accounting, and keeps players involved even when it's not their turn.

Strategy: Players should make meaningful decisions in the game that determine whether they win or lose in the end, and there should be several different winning strategies possible. It shouldn't never feel like two computers could be playing the game with the same result.

An interesting theme: Hobby games publishers have limited advertising budgets, so their games must "sell themselves." Your game should grab customers' attention while surrounded by other games on a retail shelf, perhaps with an "edgy" or humorous theme, or a unique shtick. Purely abstract games are more common in the educational market; add a unique backstory to sell your otherwise-abstract game to a hobby games publisher.

An immersive experience: Players should imagine they're part of the backstory, and feel personally invested in the game. Win or lose, they should become attached to their avatar and in-game accomplishments.

Interrelated theme and rules: The theme and rules should evoke each other in integral and complementary ways, not just be slapped together for convenience's sake. Identify the most important or unique parts of your backstory, and develop rules to emphasize them.

Solid rules and mechanics: Submissions should be playtested and edited, their rules should be complete and easy to follow, with no broken mechanics. A publisher can forgive rough graphic design, but will reject a game if its rules aren't at a professional level. Before you send your prototype, ask a group of new players to figure out your game, and watch without answering questions. It's very enlightening.

Innovative rules: Publishers look for new concepts, not variations on what's been done. Poker or chess variants, or re-themed versions of *Risk* won't get you anywhere. And your submission shouldn't be just another combat game. Publishers want designers with original ideas.

Innovative components: This includes things like transparent cards or pre-painted miniatures. Innovation breaks out of the mold that leaves so many games looking alike, and adds visual interest that sells games as much as an interesting theme does.

Easily manufactured components: Conversely, it's easiest for a publisher to produce a game with a format they've used before. Components new to them—like pre-painted miniatures—require researching new suppliers. They might do this for truly innovative designs, but balancing innovation with ease of production is important.

Compatibility with other products: The game should complement your publisher's other game lines, without competing with them. The publisher should immediately see how your game fits their existing product mix when reading your proposal. This is where targeting publishers is important.

The correct target market: Hobby games publishers like games that fit the product mix of specialty game stores, because they have well-established distribution there. They like it better if games appeal to other markets, like the book trade or mass market, since that increases sales.

A good title: The title should be unique, memorable, evocative of the theme, and appealing to its core market. Brainstorm, and ask the opinion of friends who fit your target demographics. Then do a web search, including the Trademark Electronic Search System (TESS) of the U.S. Patent and Trademark Office, to verify that your frontrunner isn't taken; your publisher will trademark it later. Also, the name must be pronounceable; a customer won't ask for it if he embarrasses himself trying.

Expansion potential: If the game succeeds, it should be possible to prduce expansions. Keep a list of cards and rules that didn't make it into the original game, for use later.

Multi-language capability: Games with no English words on the cards or pieces make a multi-language rulebook possible. This opens those markets and increases sales.

Easy demoing: Games that can be demonstrated in a small space, two feet by two feet, are easier to show in publishers' convention booths and to play in public spaces.

Collectibility only if really necessary: Manufacturing a collectible game costs vastly more than a noncollectible one. Collectible games also require much larger advertising investments, and nation- or world-wide infrastructure for tournaments, so many publishers aren't interested in them.

THE PROPOSAL

If you've found the perfect publisher for your game, you've verified that they're taking submissions, and you have their release form, the next step is to send a proposal before investing your time and money in sending a prototype. This applies even if the game design is already finished; a publisher won't want to review a full prototype if it resembles something they already have in the works, after all.

The ideal proposal is about one single-spaced page. It sums up your idea, and what's special about it; remember, this is your only chance to sell your design, so make it sound fun and exciting! It also contains vital information such as the time required to play, number of players needed, player age range, included components, and how much time would be required for you to produce a completed draft or prototype. An embedded image of the game components is a good idea, too, if it's likely to reflect well on the game. Your name, address, telephone number, and email address should be listed on the proposal; separate should be the release form and (optional) cover letter telling the publisher a little bit about yourself. Publishers may not mind simultaneous submissions, but be sure to tell them now if it's also being reviewed elsewhere.

Mail your proposal and release form to the publisher, unless they specifically request it be sent by email. If you want to be notified when the publisher receives the proposal, consider including a self-addressed stamped postcard that they can just throw in the mail. Most publishers won't be able to return proposals to you, so don't send anything you need back.

Now all you can do is wait. Remember that most publishers' first priority is actually making games; going through proposals is necessarily far down on their to-do list. Patience really is a virtue, in this case, since contacting them repeatedly to find out whether they've looked at your proposal yet will only annoy them.

THE PROTOTYPE SUBMISSION

Once the publisher has reviewed your proposal and decided it looks interesting, you'll be asked to send a full-length prototype. Complete submissions should be presented in a clean, professional manner. Publishers don't expect everything to be perfect, but they're interested in work that requires as little editorial effort as possible. A submission full of spelling and grammar problems will likely be rejected, since they can't afford the time to clean it up.

Art and good graphic design can really improve the overall appeal of a prototype, conveying the atmosphere of the game much better than raw text does. But remember that publishers generally prefer to commission art themselves, and may see your custom illustrations as unwanted strings attached to the game, whether you have a contract with your artist or not. Instead, temporarily use stock art that you can find with a web search, and be sure to tell your publisher you don't own the copyright on the illustrations.

You want to make the job of examining and testing your game as painless as possible. Prototypes should be pre-assembled; don't ask them to cut out cards, for example. Your name, address, telephone number, and email address should be on the front page of your submission, to make contacting you as easy as possible for them.

Again, if you send a game submission and you'd like to know that your prototype arrived safely, send a self-addressed, stamped postcard with it. If you haven't gotten an acknowledgment of receipt within two weeks of sending it, then you can get in touch with them to be sure it arrived safely; things have been known to get lost or misplaced. If you'd like the publisher to return your submission to you once they've reviewed it, include a self-addressed stamped envelope or box with correct postage.

Allow plenty of time for a publisher to review your proposal or submission; if you send a game prototype they'll want to playtest it, which could take several months. That's a long time, but on the plus side you'll sometimes get playtest comments to help you develop the game, even if they don't publish it. And there's always the chance that their response will include a contract.

RIGHTS & PAYMENT

Contracts can be intimidating. They're pretty basic when you break them down, though. You grant the publisher your copyright and the right to print, publish, distribute, and license the work. In return, they pay you. But the rights a publisher buys and the payment terms they offer varies a great deal from one publisher to the next, and even from one product to the next.

For example, if you're working on a supplement for an existing product you might be offered a flat fee for your work, or even a work-for-hire contract— one that gives all of your rights to the publisher forever, so that the publisher is actually considered the legal author rather than just licensing the work from you. If you've designed a completely new game, you could be offered royalties instead. With a flat fee, you get your money right away, usually within 30 days of signing the contract, delivery of your work, or publication (which one is specified in the contract). With a royalty—a percentage of each sale, usually paid quarterly and based on suggested retail price or some other per-unit measure—you have the possibility of sharing the profits if the game is a success, but you're also taking on part of the risk, too, since if the game fails you don't get paid.

To put these payment terms in perspective, remember that your publisher only gets a fraction of the retail price of each game. They usually sell the game to distributors for 40% of the retail price (who then sell to retailers for 50% to 60% of retail), and manufacturing the game costs at least 10% of the retail price if not more. Your publisher also has to pay all the people involved in producing your game, for their equipment and office space, and for advertising, warehousing, and shipping costs, and they have to come out at the end with a profit of some kind. And if they're selling to certain markets, like to the book trade, they also have the risk of returnability if the games don't sell.

In addition to payment terms, most contracts include requirements that:

- You warrant that the game hasn't been published previously, that it's your own original work, and that you own all rights to it (much like you attested to in the release form).
- You grant the publisher the right to develop the game and edit for spelling, grammar, style, and content.
- You grant the publisher reprint rights.
- You grant the publisher subsidiary rights (electronic, radio, TV, movie, merchandising, and translation rights), which they can then license to someone else if they like.
- You promise to deliver the game content by a particular due date and according to a scope of work, which specifies word count and components that you're responsible for supplying the publisher.

Publishers usually use a boilerplate that's written to address all of their legal concerns, and often have standard payment terms they offer to designers without much room for negotiation on the base fee or royalty. There are some things you can ask for that can make the contract more attractive for you:

- A royalty that increases after the first couple thousand copies are sold.
- A higher royalty on subsidiary rights.
- An advance on your royalty so that you're guaranteed some payment for your time.
- A lot of complimentary copies or a discount on your own future purchases of your product; if you attend game conventions, this might

become a good income stream for you if you can sell them yourself for a profit.

- An electronic copy of the product, if it will be released for sale as such.
- Right of approval for edits and for the final product.
- The option to design revisions, expansions, and sequels yourself, and to approve any such designed by someone else.
- Cover credit, so that your name appears not only in the credits as the designer, but also prominently on the box.

And you should always make absolutely certain that there's a reversion of rights clause, so that after a certain amount of time out of print—usually one year—you get all of your rights to the game back and can find a new publisher.

A contract is a sign that you're well on your way to getting your game published. But a lot can happen between contract and published game. Next comes the development process.

DEVELOPMENT AND EDITING

Don't fall in love with your own game; "development" in large part means doing the revisions your editor tells you to do. If not to the letter, you at least need to address each of her concerns in some way. Usually that means making a change suggested by your editor, while other times you might just need to explain why you designed it that way on purpose and get your editor's okay. An editor's job is in part to make you think through all the aspects of your game's design, and ensure there aren't better options you've overlooked. If you can think of a comparable or better way to make a fix than the one suggested by your editor, and you present your idea persuasively, she'll most often give you the artistic freedom to do it your way. Your editor is likely only going to give you one chance to fix everything, then she'll change it herself. So take your editor's revision comments for what they are, constructive criticism from an experienced source, and approach them with a positive attitude. After all, an appreciated editor is a happy editor.

The first revision you'll be asked to do will likely be based on the playtest your publisher did before accepting your submission; in fact, you might be required to do this revision before you're given your contract. The editor you'll be working with on the project will send you a list of the comments and questions that the playtest generated, and give you a deadline for revising the game. This is going to be a rude awakening for you. You're going to read this really excessively long list of comments, none of which are phrased in a particularly sensitive way, and take it personally. But remember, your publisher likes your game, or wouldn't have promised to publish it. Revisions are just the polish that turns a good game into a great game, but most games have room for a lot of polish.

After your first revision, the game will be sent out for a full round of playtesting with several experienced groups that your publisher has trained. Some publishers invite you to be a part of this process, likely leading one of the playtest groups. In this case, you and your players will be given a non-disclosure agreement to sign, which is just your promise not to tell anyone outside of your playtest group about the product.

Playtesting usually takes about a month or two. At the end of this time, your editor will either give you her summary of what she feels are the relevant points from the playtest reports (edited for designer consumption), or she'll give you the raw playtest reports themselves. A playtest report summarizes the consensus of the group on the merits and flaws of the playtest materials. There's usually an overview of the most notable strong points and deficiencies in the playtest materials. Then a section-by-section breakdown is the meat of the report; for example, it might comment on the overall rules and each card of a card or board game separately. General comments not connected to a specific section are often given at the end of the report.

The thing to remember about raw playtest reports is that they're not all created equal. Some playtesters are "rules lawyers" and will pick apart the rules, while others will take a more holistic approach and just describe their play experience in emotive terms. Some playtest groups may even be filled with people who aren't your target audience, who don't "get" the game and so are overly harsh, or who have a hard time just admitting they didn't have fun. Think of the likely result of a diehard WWII miniatures gamer playtesting *Apples to Apples*, playing to win rather than to have a fun social experience. He'd probably decide it was fundamentally broken, and miss the point of the game. If the report lists demographics of the playtesters like age and gender, preferred types of games or occupation, be sure to note this and weigh the report accordingly. Don't take a playtest report the same way you would your editor's critique; be sure you're seeing the forest for the trees.

Once you've waded through these reports and your playtest revision is in, your editor will do a close edit of the game. This is the nitpicky stuff, like smoothing out the wording on the cards and rules for easy understanding, and editing for consistency. Your editor will probably tell you what she's changed in editing, but may not give you another chance for revision at this point.

WHAT MAKES GOOD RULES?

Good card and board game rules usually have some common elements. They use lots of subheaders for easy reference, and they include:

Overview: Start with an exciting first line to get potential buyers interested, say what type of game it is (abstract, storytelling, combat, etc.), give a quick overview of basic game play, and a mention of the win condition so players know what their goal is from the start.

Components: Give a list of components, including the number and type of cards and other pieces included in the game. Also, mention the components the players need to provide for themselves, like a watch for keeping time, or paper and pencil for tracking scores, or pennies as tokens. This is also a good place to note the number and recommended ages of players, and the time required to play.

Setup: Describe how to sort and shuffle the cards, what and how many cards are dealt for player hands, whether players can look at their hands, where the draw deck(s) go after dealing, and whether cards on the table are face up or down. Also mention if discard piles will form during play, and where they should go. Any other components in the game should be mentioned here, with specifics on how many are distributed to players and where the extras go. Name the starting player (a clever theme-appropriate choice is always more fun).

Gameplay: Define "turn" and "round" if you're using alternate terms (though this is only suggested if they relate directly to the theme of the game and don't become confusing), describe turn rotation briefly (alternating turns, simultaneous turns, etc.), list player turn actions in order, then describe them in detail. An insert box with a bullet list of actions in order is always a good reference to include here.

Card types: Identify each card type, then think about these questions: When is each card type played? Where does the card come from? Where does it go after it's played? Are there any card interactions that should be described in special detail? What if you run out of cards in the draw pile? This is also a good place for a diagram of the play space and some sample card illustrations with labels.

Endgame and winning: Describe how to tally up scores and determine who wins. Including a clever theme-related reward for the winner, like the title "The Great Dalmuti," lets players end their game experience on a positive note.

Example of play/strategy hints/optional rules/game variants/ glossary: Use the extra sections that you need, but no more. A rules-heavy game might include them all, but a rules-light game is likely better off putting these on the publisher's website as free downloads. They generally make the rules look more complicated and intimidating than they need to for first-time players.

Credits: List yourself as the game designer, include the names of all of your playtesters, and add a "special thanks" line if you'd like to acknowledge someone for their contributions. Also claim a copyright on the rules and a trademark on your title. You can do this simply by writing "©(year) (Your Name). (Your Game Title) is a trademark of (Your Name). All rights reserved." Your publisher will add the rest of the credits as part of the production process.

PRODUCTION

Your game will be assigned a project manager, who may or may not be the same editor you had before, depending on the size and internal structure of your publisher. In addition to guiding you through your part of the development process—mainly playtesting and revisions—she's also in charge of the rest of the production process for your game, including art direction, graphic design, layout, proofreading, pre-press, and printing/manufacturing. She's often also responsible for developing marketing and advertising materials like sell text. Some publishers will assign your project a separate art director and layout artist.

Your part of all of this—after sending your submission prototype, negotiating your contract, and doing revisions—is to provide your publisher with the reworked materials for your game. These usually include a list of components, the revised rules and cardlist, and often your art suggestions. Art suggestions usually have three parts: diagrams, cover art, and interior art. Diagrams are required of the designer, while cover art and interior art suggestions are often optional.

For diagrams you'll want to provide a sketch of the layout of each of your card types, and a good drawing of your game board. A big part of a game board is often a detailed map of something like a country, city, building plan, dungeon, or cave. It doesn't need to be a work of art itself; a rough sketch is enough, but you should be aware of a few things:

- Sketches should be legible.
- They should have important elements labeled, and include descriptive text so the cartographer knows what each area looks like and how it functions.
- The sketches should also have scale measurements noted, and mention if a grid overlay is necessary.
- Provide images or web links as reference for the artist, especially if the map is of a real-life area or structure.
- Work to the print size of your board; if you overcrowd it, no one will be able to read the labels.

The cover art and the interior art suggestions usually describe a scene; for cover art it's one that represents your game as a whole, while interior art for the cards and rulebook focuses on illustrating a particular aspect of the game. Your editor probably won't be able to use all your suggestions, but writing good art descriptions increases your chances. Also, keep in mind that art is an expensive part of production, so if your game won't suffer for using multiples of some cards, mention that to your editor in development. Here are several other things you'll want to consider:

- Designers and artists almost never talk directly, so this description is all the artist is going to have to go on. Make it count with detailed descriptions when they're needed, but also remember that artists feel overwhelmed by too much cut-and-pasted text and are likely to overlook important specifics.
- Each piece should have a reason for being included; is it to illustrate what a creature or place or item looks like, or maybe just to establish a particular atmosphere? Let the artist know what your intent is for the illustration, to help him decide what's important to include in it.
- The best art has action, rather than being just a character portrait or still life, and it focuses on the parts of the game that are truly unique.
- Consider elements like time of day, descriptions of clothing and items, backgrounds (having no background is called a "vignette"), body pose including what characters are holding and where their hands are, and facial expression.
- Things like point of view and composition can also be specified if they're important, but remember that these choices are usually the purview of the artist; allow him creative freedom whenever possible.
- Whenever possible, include women and a variety of races (orcs and elves don't count) in your art suggestions.
- Try not to require more than three central figures in any one piece. An entire army usually doesn't fit in a single illustration.
- Also consider that the artist is going to have trouble depicting things like sound, smell, or color (when working in greyscale), and extremely subtle feelings.
- Include images or web links to examples of things like period dress or architectural styles.

Don't forget to add descriptions of the symbols or icons your game needs, as well as card borders, card backs, character markers, punch-out tokens, and any other game pieces that are illustrated.

Once it's been assigned, art can take several months to complete, depending on how many illustrations the project requires and how many artists are working on it. Layout can take just as long, but the two are often able to be done at the same time. Things will take more time if your project manager is working on more than one game, though. But eventually it gets one last proofread, then the final files are sent the printer to be made into an actual physical game.

A few weeks later, you may be asked to approve proofs that the printer provides to your publisher (especially if you negotiated right of approval in your contract). Proofs of cards are sent as a press sheet; for example, 110 poker-sized cards may be printed on one large sheet of cardstock, with dielines printed where they'll be cut out. Tuckboxes and softcovers for books are also printed on press sheets, generally several to one sheet. Other parts of your game, like tokens or game boards, might be submitted as mockups that actually look exactly as they will when printed. Or the printer might provide a PDF proof instead, for you to approve on-screen. Whatever the proofs look like, be sure to return them to your publisher immediately. At this point, you're very close to the release deadline for the game, and no one can afford for approvals to take much time.

RELEASE

Your game is back from the printer and will hit stores any day now. Now you're a superstar! Well, not really, but there are some public relations-related things your publisher will need you to do as the creator of the game. For example, you might be asked to do interviews by email or phone with industry magazines, websites, or podcasts. You may need to answer rules questions, both on the publisher's online discussion forum and for any customer service emails forwarded to you. If problems or enough questions arise, you'll need to provide your publisher with answers for a FAQ or errata sheet for their website. And your publisher may invite you to game conventions where they have an exhibitor booth, so you can do demos of your game and possibly signings. Or maybe you'll even be asked to attend as a guest of honor of the convention, if your game becomes popular enough.

It's taken two years or more from proposal to printed product, but you've done it...you've gotten your game professionally published in the hobby games industry!

Michelle Nephew *is the designer of the transparent card game Ren Faire from Atlas Games. She's also the head of game production for Atlas, where she has edited dozens of card games, board games, and RPG books. Michelle has her Ph.D. in English Literature, with her dissertation on the topic of authorship and roleplaying games.*

Afterword

In editing rules written by many designers, I've noticed that the section they most often forget to include is the Object of the Game. They'll launch right into Components and Gameplay and Exceptions to the Exceptions, and remember to tell you how to win only after they've inundated you with activities whose rationales you do not yet understand. I remind them how much easier it is to grok a game when you know why you're playing it.

Which doesn't excuse me for making such a rookie mistake with this book.

In my foreword, I could easily have given you an Object of the Book. It would have read something like this: To be the designer with the best practical understanding of how to make a good game. There. That's a pretty great goal. You want to win that game.

Here's the thing: Even if you take all these essays to heart, you're probably not winning that game any time soon. That's because the people who wrote these words have been living them their entire lives. We wouldn't be writing those words if we hadn't experimented and modified and codified our approaches over the decades.

The thing is, now you know what we know. But we don't know what you know. Not yet, anyway. Game designers are inherently collaborative; we draw ideas out of each other, and we form our ideas around those of our friends. If you know what you're doing, you can contribute to that discussion. Just like we can make your games better, you can make our games better. Find us at a convention, and try us out. As Teeuwynn described, if you're "outgoing, articulate, and analytically minded enough," you'll fit in nicely.

Even with all this information we've just wedged into your head, there's a couple more notes I'd like to give you. These are meta-points, designed to not only get you further along toward the Object of the Book, but also to make you practically suited to having a long career in the game industry.

First, slow down. I know that the most powerful force in a game designer's life is the desire to be done with something. Resist that force. Let your game take the time it needs to be great. A game is only late once, but it's bad forever.

Second, speed up. You might believe that there's no such thing as a bad idea in a brainstorm, or a playtest that's complete before the game is played all the way through. This is foolery. There are plenty of bad ideas and plenty of bad playtests. You don't have time for that nonsense. Politely move your process along so that you can get more good results efficiently.

Third, don't try to be us. There are a lot of great designers in here, and each of us is something different from each other. Be who you are, and your games will mold themselves to your personality. Unless you don't have a personality, in which case you should invent one. But I'm guessing you do. Find an identity, and people will want all your games.

Fourth, write games you want to play. I don't mean that you are your target audience for your games; you're not. But find something in every game you want to show off over and over again. Preferably multiple things. If you enjoy demoing your game, people will enjoy playing it.

Finally, when you've absorbed all of this, and after you've published a ton of games according to a set of design principles that you've assimilated and altered and beaten into shape, don't just sit there. Write your own damn book.

Because that's a book I want to read. My friends might too.

Thanks for reading ours.

Mike Selinker

Seattle, Washington

Made in the USA
Middletown, DE
17 October 2015